BIVOCATIONAL

BIVOCATIONAL

RETURNING TO THE ROOTS OF MINISTRY

MARK D. W. EDINGTON

Church Publishing
NEW YORK

Church Publishing
19 East 34th Street
New York, NY 10016
www.churchpublishing.org

Cover design by Paul Soupiset
Typeset by PerfecType, Nashville, Tennessee

A record of this book is available from the Library of Congress.

ISBN-13: 978-0-8192-3386-8 (pbk.)
ISBN-13: 978-0-8192-3387-5 (ebook)

Printed in the United States of America

. . . you have made them to be a kingdom and priests serving our God, and they will reign on earth.

—Revelation 5:10

Contents

For my Fellow Ministers in Saint John's, Newtonville

οὐ παύομαι εὐχαριστῶν ὑπὲρ ὑμῶν,
μνείαν ὑμῶν ποιούμενος ἐπὶ τῶν προσευχῶν μου
—Ephesians 1:16

Introduction

In Team 63 at C. E. MacDonald Middle School in East Lansing, Michigan, the sixth-grade math and science teacher was a fellow named Jerry Smith. Mr. Smith lives for me in the category of teachers you remember long after most of the rest of the parade of instructors who passed in front of the classrooms you sat in have been forgotten. He expected a lot out of us, but his class was engaging, intriguing, and just occasionally a place of wonder.

Even more impressive to this sixth-grade boy, he was a pilot—and not just any sort of pilot; he had flown C-47s in the Canadian Air Force and held ratings as a multiengine aircraft pilot and as an instructor. He even had aviator glasses and a goatee. To me and to most of my friends, Jerry Smith was the epitome of cool.

Pretty much every boy in the middle school wanted to be in his class when, every other week, we had "flex time"—alternative classes the teachers offered to broaden our horizons. There were classes in macramé and origami, pottery and ballroom dancing (thanks, no). Mr. Smith offered an hour-long class in aviation and navigation—which was pretty much the only thing I wanted to do during flex time. He brought in aeronautical charts and taught us how to plot flight paths accounting for the speed and direction of prevailing winds and the variations between true north and magnetic north. We used (no kidding) circular slide rules called E6Bs, straight edges, and pencils to plan endless trips we never made from St. Louis to Denver, from Phoenix to Santa Fe, from Baltimore to Tampa.

Of course, he never told us that the whole point was to get us to learn trigonometry. We didn't care. We were completely fascinated by the idea of airplanes.

Jerry Smith was a marvelous and creative teacher. He was also an Episcopal priest. He served as the part-time vicar of the little mission church in Williamston, Michigan, a town about ten miles to the east of where I grew up. Most kids can't imagine the lives their teachers have in the hours they don't spend in the classroom; for Jerry Smith, it was the life of ordained ministry.

I only learned after I was out of sixth grade that Jerry Smith was also Pastor Jerry. I didn't go to church in Williamston, so I never saw him there. Instead, a couple of years or so later he came to my church when we were instituting a new rector, and for the first time I saw him in a clerical collar. I was completely floored. But somehow I wasn't surprised. To me, he was still Mr. Smith—a great teacher with a gift for engaging kids and getting them to learn even when they thought they were doing something else.

I have thought a lot about Mr. Smith in the years since I was ordained, after first pursuing a graduate degree and a research career. I wonder how he managed to keep the balance between the steep demands public school teachers manage (something I grew up knowing, because my mom was one, too) and the needs of his parish. I have come to see that the people of his parish had to have been a big part of making it work, just as the people of my parish have been more than half the equation of creating our own kind of bivocational ministry.

But mostly I think back to that flex-time class because, in a lot of ways, it held the key to Jerry Smith's success, not just as a teacher but as a person called to the ministry of the church—and as a Christian who lived his ministry not just in the church, but in the world. Jerry Smith knew how to capture our imagination and our interests. I thought I was exploring my fascination with flying; in fact, I was learning math. He translated my curiosity into exploration—which is, after all, what lies at the heart of the call to witness that all members of the church have. By engaging my curiosity about airplanes, he taught me something about trigonometry. By affirming my interests and channeling my enthusiasm, he helped me realize my gifts. But, of course, for Jerry Smith that wasn't just what teachers do; it was, in no small way, the cornerstone of what ministry is, no matter who is doing it.

This is a book about bivocational ministry. In some ways the idea that ministry is bivocational may seem like a statement of the obvious; each of us who shares in the ministry of the baptized is meant to carry out that ministry in the world, and not merely in the church. But in some ways it is profoundly countercultural, at least in terms of traditional church culture, because it imagines a different way of structuring the ministry of the faith community, parish, or congregation, from the model we have received.

Most of us grew up with the model that ordained ministers are people who "have a vocation," and who serve the church in a *profession* called ordained ministry. Many if not most of us still regard that idea—consciously or unconsciously—as normative. Like all professions, the ordained ministry is characterized by specialized knowledge and a set of institutions for transmitting that knowledge (divinity schools and seminaries). It has systems for credentialing those who are approved to become part of the profession (usually a qualifying examination and a rite of ordination), standards of professional conduct (a book of discipline, canon laws), and expectations for participation in the profession (continuing education, participation in regular meetings of clergy).

Those who become admitted to this profession receive certain benefits by means of being credentialed. First, they have a particular kind of authority within their church. To cite specifics, in some churches only ordained people can preach, can read from the gospels at the time of Holy Communion, can pronounce a blessing or absolve people of confessed sins, or can perform certain other sacramental acts. In churches of Protestant persuasion this authority is generally held in balance by a democratically governed congregation, or by the expectation of obedience to a bishop or polity—or both. Members of the profession are also entitled to certain privileges created by custom (for example, the honorific "The Reverend") or by law (in most states ordained people may still function as civil authorities in solemnizing marriages).

Members of the ministerial profession are typically given exclusive access to certain sorts of jobs within the church. One must be ordained not just to exercise certain kinds of spiritual authority, but to be employed in certain jobs within the structure of a given polity: a pastor, a senior minister, a rector. Being chosen for one of these jobs means a salary, general participation in a retirement program, and access to health insurance.

So our model of ministry, at least since the late 1800s, has been one of professionalization. That, in turn, has had a formative impact on our notion of what "church" is. Among other things, a church is a social institution that has an ordained professional as its leader. And that has some particular economic implications as well: a church is an economic entity that can afford to hire a full-time professional as its leader. That's pretty much what we mean when we call something a "church."

It is no accident that this general notion of how the church is (or should be) structured arose during the period of industrial organization—which itself happened in parts of the world significantly shaped by Protestant ideas. Theorists today speak of this as one of three basic ways of organizing human communities to produce things humans need: it is "firm-based production." Firm-based production is a way of organizing to produce goods—not necessarily material goods, but cultural or spiritual goods as well—that depends on a hierarchical structure best suited to a centralized decision-making process. Market-based production, by contrast, uses the incentives and signals of the market to encourage creativeness, invention, and efficient distribution. Markets produce things in a decentralized way, while firms do best in areas where centralization and hierarchy confer advantages.[1] (I'll get to the third alternative in a little while.)

Of course, the hierarchy of the church existed long before the emergence of industrial economies. In virtually all expressions of the Christian community—Catholic, Orthodox, Protestant—a hierarchical structure has been seen as both grounded in scripture and essential to the maintenance of doctrinal discipline. Hierarchical structures facilitated the kind of centralized decision-making that made possible the global spread of different expressions of the Christian message; the building of universities, schools, and hospitals; and even the creation of the ecumenical movement. But the strong emphasis that industrial economic development gave to both hierarchical structures and the dominant role of professions in shaping the leadership of those structures has had a profound impact on our understanding of what the church is and does. The ministry, one of the three ancient "learned professions" (along with medicine and law), became a *modern* profession—an occupational specialization with attendant structures, expectations, and privileges.

To get a sense of the true scale of that impact, think for a moment about other parts to our model of ministry—things seemingly so obvious we don't really think about them. A church not only has a full-time

---

1. Yochai Benkler, *The Wealth of Networks: How Social Production Transforms Markets and Freedom* (New Haven, Conn.: Yale University Press, 2006).

ordained minister as its leader; it typically has a building of its own. It may also have a residential building that is kept to house the minister—something that has long been understood to be both a benefit to the minister and a matter of convenience for the congregation. (Members of other professions, especially in government and academe, sometimes receive a similar benefit.) Typically it has a parish house or church hall, a function room where activities of the community can take place. All of this property, under our current model, is given privileged treatment by the civil authorities—specifically, it has been exempted from taxation for most purposes.

And there are other, less obvious, parts of our model of ministry. Often, the children of ordained ministers have been given discounted tuition at private schools and colleges. Ministers and their families were often welcomed at different sorts of social clubs for a discounted fee. And it is still the case that members of the clergy may write a letter to the front office of the Boston Red Sox in the late winter of each year to receive a pass to Fenway Park, assuring them a place in the standing-room-only section—alongside members of the armed services—for a relatively small price.

The power of this model of ministry—let's call it the "Standard Model"—has shaped not just the economic arrangements that underlie what we think of as "church"; it has shaped much of what we understand to be involved in the practice of ministry and congregational leadership. Under the Standard Model, we expect the minister to be not just the chief spiritual officer of the community, but the chief operating officer of a non-profit, tax-exempt corporation. We expect the professional minister to administer a staff of varying sizes, or to perform the functions of what needed staff might do in a small parish. We expect the professional minister to be the public face and voice of the congregation within the community it serves. We expect the professional minister to be the first responder to the spiritual and pastoral needs of the parish, to manage business relationships on the part of the church with contractors and vendors, and to interact with municipal authorities on topics from parking spaces and garbage collection to low-income housing and food and fuel assistance for the poor.

Said in different terms, we expect our professional ministers to exercise more than spiritual leadership with the congregation. We expect them to discharge a variety of delegated responsibilities that have more to do with running the business of an entity called "the church" than with any theologically grounded understanding of the distinctive gifts and distinctive roles of those set apart by the body of Christ—the community of the faithful—to exercise a distinct sort of ministry, an ordained ministry, for and within the church. The Standard Model looks a lot like firm-based production. It is organized hierarchically in order to support centralized decision-making in an institution that provides spiritual services to its members and the broader community. Exactly because we are pooling our resources to pay our professional ministers, we expect them to do everything from running the worship service to fixing the copier machine, maintaining the web page, showing up at the affordable-housing hearing, dealing with the nursery school renting space in the basement, and—oh, yes—visiting the folks on the at-home list, teaching us about the faith, attracting new members, and making us want to be better people.

If you are reading this book, chances are you are aware that many of the assumptions—explicit and implicit—on which the Standard Model of ministry were based are now under tremendous pressure. For some of us, it feels as though the very stones in our foundation are giving way; where once all was certainty, now the world of the church seems a realm of instability, decline, and loss. Certainly the privileged treatment of churches and faith communities once typical in our society—expressed not just through favored treatment in law and tax code but by school calendars, shopping hours, and countless other expressions of deference to Christian values— is ending. With the collapse of much of this favored treatment has come a rise in the sheer cost of doing the work of the church. To say it in other words, the basic assumptions of our business model are changing. Simply maintaining a full-time, fully benefitted professional as the head of the organization known as "the church" is increasingly something beyond the resources of more and more congregations.[2]

---

2. A major change may be coming in the basic costs of the Standard Model. A number of recent cases in federal court have challenged the constitutionality of 26 U.S.C. § 107(2)—the law that exempts clergy housing allowances from taxation. After an initial ruling in the Western District of Wisconsin striking down the provision was vacated on appeal, a second case was brought—and, again, the decision at the district court has been to declare the provision unconstitutional, "because it does not have a secular purpose or effect and because a reasonable observer would view the statute as an endorsement [by the federal government] of religion." Gaylor vs. Mnuchin, United States District Court for the Western District of Wisconsin, Case 3:16-cv-215-bbc, decided October 6, 2017.

To understand why this decision has significant impact on parish finances, imagine a senior minister in a congregation who is paid $80,000 per year, of which she has asked $24,000 to be paid as a housing allowance. She would have to be able to show that her actual housing costs—her rental payment, or the rental value of a home she uses the funds to pay a mortgage with, together with utility costs—are at least $2,000 per month; but in most American cities that would not be hard to do, especially if she has a home that must accommodate a family. Let's also say that she's the only wage earner in her home, that she's married and filing jointly with her spouse, and that they have no dependent children at home.

Under the recently revised tax law, the minister's taxable income for 2018 would be $56,000 per year; the $24,000 she receives in housing allowance would not be taxed. Assuming, just to make this simple, that she has no other exemptions, she would pay $3,459 in federal income taxes. But if the housing allowance were ended, her taxable income would now be $80,000—which would mean she would now pay $6,339 in federal income taxes. The net impact of this would be a decrease in her income (because of a rise in taxes) of $2,880—or an effective cut of 3.6 percent in her total earnings. (Remember, she still has to pay her rent.) Needless to say, the effect of this will be to raise the bar on the average cost to a congregation of maintaining a full-time professional minister—our Standard Model—and to increase the number of congregations confronting a difficult decision about their future.

So here is the hard truth: the question many congregations face today is whether this professional model of ministry is consistent with their future, or with them *having* a future. Because we have equated a vocation to ministry with membership in a profession called "the ministry," and because the Standard Model of ministry expects that a congregation must have a full-time member of that profession to be a viable church, we have created a set of economic circumstances that are causing a great many congregations to make hard choices. Will we have to close? Will we have to merge with another congregation across town, or maybe in the next town over? Or maybe—just maybe—might we reimagine the model of ministry we have inherited from the generations of faithful people before us?

Other Choices, Other Models

Of course, the expectations of the Standard Model are far more a result of choices that we have made—or that our ancestors made—than they are a theological necessity. As I said, we have created these expectations. And that means we could create a different set of expectations by making a different set of choices. So while it might cause us some discomfort, exploring the full range of choices in structuring new models of ministry might just open new possibilities for flourishing in the faith communities we love. That is the opportunity before us. And while it may feel disorienting, it may even be that there is something in it of God's hope for us.

A first step some congregations have already taken to relieve economic pressure is to move toward a *part-time* model of ministry. A number of conditions have to be in place for this to work. The congregation has to be of such size and scale that a part-time professional minister can cover the needed tasks. Because this model is usually premised on an assumption that the basic division of labor between the ordained and lay members of the congregation remains substantially unchanged, the size of the congregation and of its associated work—liturgical, pastoral, administrative, and social—has to match the availability of the minister.

At the same time, the part-time model imposes an implied expectation that the minister chosen by the congregation will have other financial resources on which to survive. A working spouse or partner—or perhaps a trust fund—will provide the resources for that minister's health insurance and retirement investment plan. The congregation may provide much the same support to the part-time minister as they would to a full-time minister in terms of expense reimbursements—for travel, say, or perhaps for a car or a telephone—but the elements of a total compensation plan that increasingly drive costs (for example, health care and retirement, and potentially housing) are managed in this model simply by being avoided.

A second alternative model is to unite two or more parishes into a model often labeled *shared* ministry. In a shared ministry model, the resources of a number of congregations are combined so as to preserve, and thus work in service of, the basic outlines of the Standard Model of ministry: a full-time, fully benefited professional who, in this case, serves more than one parish.

The shared ministry model is even more likely to be based on the same essential concepts as the Standard Model because the central orienting concept of a shared ministry approach is the preservation of a full-time position for an appropriately qualified and certified professional. (Indeed, you could say that the shared ministry model is basically a preservation program for the full-time professional model of ministry.) For this reason, the basic division of responsibilities between the ordained professional and the lay members of the congregations gathered together in this ministry is—as in the part-time model—unlikely to change in substantial ways. The ordained professional will still be looked to for performing traditional roles and responsibilities within the congregation. The basic change that members of each of the participating communities will need to work through centers on appropriately calibrating their expectations of the pastor's time for the needs of *their* congregation, given that *other* congregations also have a claim on the pastor's time as well. Success in a model of shared ministry depends in large part on creating effective governance structures able to clarify the shared expectations of each congregation participating in the arrangement—to make certain they cohere together and do not end up creating an impossible set of demands.

Both the part-time model and the shared model of ministry can be made to work, and in many places they are already doing so. This book does not address either of those models. Instead it focuses on a third, very different model—that of *bivocational* ministry.

Bivocational ministry begins with a different set of assumptions, and ends with a different understanding of how the church can be structured to do its work of ministry. First, in a bivocational congregation the ordained minister works both in the church and, in some way, in the secular world. This latter role may be easily imagined as an outgrowth of pastoral ministry—say, working as a social worker or therapist, or perhaps in a leadership role within a non-profit agency. Like my old teacher Mr. Smith, the minister's job in the secular world may be as a public-sector employee—a teacher, or perhaps an administrator or public defender. Or it may be in a different form of self-employment—say, as a consultant or a real-estate agent. Typically, one result of this arrangement will be that the minister's access to health insurance and a retirement plan are provided through the secular employer, or through an individual policy for which the congregation provides some limited support.

But it is not only the ordained minister in a bivocational parish who is bivocational. In fact, in the optimal realization of this model *the entire congregation adopts a bivocational understanding of the ministry it is called to do in the world.* This is not just an accidental byproduct of the sort of person a congregation hires; it is an intentional outcome of a purposeful process.

In a bivocational church, the historically rigid division between ordained responsibilities and lay roles is instead understood as different expressions of the *same* ministry—one in which *all* are now understood to be ministers of the congregation. Not surprisingly, in a bivocational congregation, the whole idea of what the church is, and what it is for, begins to change.

This sort of language is often heard in congregational life, but in the bivocational congregation it takes on a new and vivid reality. The first step in creating an effective bivocational model is typically to lift up and articulate some of the basic (and often unspoken) expectations we have of our ministers—and that ministers have of their congregations. Through this exercise congregations discover and make plain how much the Standard Model has shaped their expectations of people who serve the church in ordained ministry—and how many, if not most, of those expectations can be held up to the light of inquiry once they are brought to the surface.

A second step is to identify new ways in which these expectations can be taken on by other people in the congregation—people who may, more often than not, be better equipped for these roles than an ordained professional ever would be. An architect in the pews is probably going to be a better person to take on the work of evaluating and dealing with contractors undertaking an accessibility project. A family living with a child on the autism spectrum will probably be better and more effective advocates for community-housing opportunities for adults with autism-spectrum disorder on behalf of the congregation. And no one should have a monopoly on pastoral visitations with the sick, the elderly, and the marginalized, although that is often exactly the pattern followed in the Standard Model.

The ordained minister in a bivocational model accordingly needs a different set of skills, and even a different understanding and practice of leadership, in order for this model to flourish. In this model, something much more like "servant-leadership"—a phrase often used but rarely exemplified in a hierarchical, firm-like church culture—is not just desirable, but necessary. The ordained member of the community now has as a first task the identification, development, and encouragement of the various gifts for ministry that exist in all members of the community—and in those who come to the community to explore their faith.

This means that in a bivocational model of ministry, something about the very nature of the community itself must undergo a shift from what is, in the Standard Model, typically a *consumer* or *recipient* ethos to a *participant* or *stakeholder* ethos. This is a critical point that we'll develop more fully in chapter 2, but, for now, a brief description will point the way forward.

We said earlier that theorists have described three basic ways of shaping organizations for providing the things people need. The market is one; firms are another. Markets do well at things like building carts and growing vegetables; firms do well at things like creating bus companies and airlines, productive work that inherently demands, and benefits from, operating at larger scale.

A third way of organizing people is by means of a commons. What's different about a commons is that it does not operate, at least not in a primary way, by means of the signals of the market (so, it's not like market-based production); and it is, in general, a non-hierarchical organization (which means it's not like firm-based production). A good way of understanding this is to think about the difference between the *Encyclopedia Britannica* and Wikipedia. The *Britannica*, in its heyday, was a classic firm-based, hierarchically structured enterprise focused on the production of a knowledge resource called an encyclopedia. It had (and still has) an editor-in-chief, an editorial board, assistant editors with responsibility for specific subject areas, a team of writers and editors, and (at least back in the day) a door-to-door sales force the size of a small army. If you sketched all this on a piece of paper, you'd see something that looked pretty much like a pyramid.

A commons is different. Wikipedia is produced by a commons. It has a relatively tiny organization, and a vast number of contributors with very little structure defining their relationships to one another. What makes the production of Wikipedia possible is that the thousands of people who have generated content for it are *united by a shared passion and commitment* to the goal of providing a resource for everyone, and a shared set of values and norms for how they do their collective work. That is what a commons is, and how it works. One of the most hopeful things to happen to the Christian church in a long time is that the church itself is now facing the challenge of becoming less like a firm, and more like a commons. That is the idea at the heart of this book.

A Church of the Commons

Bivocational communities answer this challenge head on. They do so by focusing on doing the work of the church in a way that is fundamentally based, not on a hierarchy of distinctive roles and a division of labor, but on a group of peers sharing the full variety of their gifts, contributing them on the basis of a common passion and commitment to a shared goal. In this case, the "product" we are producing is both speaking about and living in accord with the Good News of the Christian gospel. Doing that still takes human organization, and likely always will. It's just that the sort of organization best suited to our vision and our hope is changing, for the simple if inconvenient reason that the world in which we do the work of discipleship is changing.

Bivocational communities are one way of responding constructively and hopefully to that change. It may seem like they are radically different from the Standard Model that all of us grew up with, and that many of us still cherish; and, to be honest, in important ways they are. But it's equally important to remember that in the whole history of the Christian faith, our model of ministry is a pretty recent invention. Over the centuries of Christian witness, a tremendous variety of ideas for how ministry should be structured and lived out have been tried, tested, implemented, and left behind when they no longer served the purpose.

For us, the Standard Model has such paradigmatic status that we can scarcely imagine how the church could ever have been organized differently. But even in the relatively short history of the United States, our basic concept of how ministry should be structured has changed dramatically. Donald Scott has shown, for example, how being the minister of a church—at least a Protestant church—in the eighteenth century was to hold what was, in effect, a public office. The history of the American ministry in the nineteenth century is in many ways the history of a shift in the idea of ministry, as Scott calls it, "from office to profession"—the sort of modern profession that forms the core of our Standard Model.[3] The fact that it has not always been so means that it need not always remain so. We are being called to respond to the changing world around us, and to bear fruit, not sour grapes.

The Structure of this Book

The full impact of a bivocational approach to ministry touches on virtually every aspect of the Standard Model we have received from our traditions. In the chapters that follow we will look at four broad categories of the life of the church, and explore how a bivocational approach to ministry would involve significant changes in each of them.

1. The Bivocational Pastor

It may seem ironic to begin a study focused on the empowerment of all people in the church for ministry by focusing on the ordained minster. But because the Standard Model shapes so much of the financial and

---

3. Donald Scott, *From Office to Profession: The New England Ministry, 1750-1850.* 1st ed. Philadelphia: University of Pennsylvania Press, 1978.

psychological reality of parishes and congregations today, it is appropriate to begin with an examination of how a bivocational pastorate differs from other models in terms of the practical realities, personal gifts, and leadership style of the individual pastor. As with any model of ministry, the bivocational pastorate has both advantages and disadvantages. Success in building a flourishing congregation with this model depends on a clear understanding of both, and the ability to craft a transition strategy from one model to another.

At the same time, the strengths and skills brought by bivocational pastors will be different, in some important respects, than those who have traditionally been seen as fit for, or "called to," the profession of ministry. Perhaps most important, their relationship to some of the traditional privileges associated with the ministerial profession will need to change, or be different in important ways. Simply put, they will need to be less focused on what makes the ordained ministry *distinct* or *privileged* in comparison to the ministry of all baptized, and instead much more engaged with, and able to develop, the shared passion and commitment on which the success of a commons-based approach depends.

2. The Bivocational Congregation

There are significant differences in both the role of the pastor and the ethos of the congregation between the Standard Model and a bivocational model of ministry. In this chapter we will describe some of those differences, seeking to point out some of the distinguishing characteristics of a bivocational congregation and the qualities present in any Christian community that can become the foundation of such an approach to ministry. The simple truth is that a successful bivocational congregation has a different feel and a different culture than a congregation in the Standard Model of ministry. Some of those differences are positive differences, at least in the sense of what Christian discipleship is supposed to be about. But some of them are just plain countercultural. They involve a set of demands that run directly against trends in the dominant culture in which our churches operate. This chapter will outline both sets of differences and look for ways to leverage the positive elements of a bivocational faith community, so as to offer an effective witness against some of the most corrosive forces of contemporary society.

3. The Bivocational Polity

If the Standard Model of ministry has shaped our experience and understanding of our own faith community, still more has it shaped the structure and functioning of our denominational polities. Tremendous resources are devoted by these organizations to the maintenance and development of the profession of the ministry. Denominational authorities typically determine the standards for credentialing members of the ministerial profession; issue these credentials, and maintain systems for revoking them; create and implement systems for the deployment of these professionals and the development of their careers; provide pension plans for members of the profession and create means of funding them through congregational contributions; and establish the organizational principles of member congregations, many of which effectively reinforce the Standard Model.

In this chapter we'll explore how polities can create conditions favorable to the emergence of bivocational ministries and communities. We'll describe ways in which, through expanding and reorienting the standards by which candidates for ordination are selected, denominations can help provide the resources critical to the emergence of bivocational ministries as a real and substantial alternative to the Standard Model. We'll look at some of the roadblocks created by the standards by which denominations determine what a "church" is that stand in the way of the emergence of bivocational congregations, and look at ways they might be removed. We'll also look at other traditional professions that have adapted successfully to the presence of bivocational members of the profession and have encouraged their professional development, seeking lessons and ideas from other experiences that might help us understand how to build a bivocational approach to ordained ministry.

4. The Bivocational Church

Ultimately, a conversation about how best to structure the work of ministry and how to steward our resources of time, talent, and treasure most effectively for the work God calls us to do is a theological conversation. To be specific, it is a conversation about *ecclesiology*—a seminary word that is meant to summarize all the elements of our doctrine of the church and the relationship between those elements.

For some readers this may well be the least interesting chapter of the book. Yet in important ways, it is perhaps the most crucial. It starts with a basic question on which Christians are not, and never have been, of one mind: Is the church meant to be a realm separate from the world, with its own structures, processes, language, and rules? Or is the church meant to be the place through which God engages the rest of the world, seeking to draw the whole world into the reconciliation offered through Jesus Christ?

This is a crucial distinction, and a great deal hangs by it. It is often oversimplified by drawing a distinction between those who see the church as an *end* unto itself, and those who see the church as a *means* to an end. But like most oversimplifications, there is a degree of truth in this distinction that sheds light on the question. If you see the church as an institution set apart and existing for its own purposes and ends, then it's fairly likely you will see our willingness to adapt to the church's needs and expectations as the means to that end. The church in this model is a source and symbol of permanence and unchanging standards, a reflection of the unchanging and transcendent nature of God.

Conversely, if you see the church as the means, then probably it is people themselves—or their engagement with the loving, transforming work of Christ—who are the end in view. The church in this model is *simply* a means—a beautiful, blessed, beloved means, but a means nonetheless—by which God seeks to achieve the end of relationship with all people. And if the means we have developed—the models we have constructed—for doing this are no longer effective, then God will dispense with them and build new ones, whether we like it or not. The church in this model is an instrument more than an objective. It is part of the continuing incarnation of God in the body of Christ, the church; but like any body, it must grow and change if it is to remain vital.

These are two very broadly defined views of what the church is and does. One is institutional, one is incarnational. Needless to say, perhaps, a bivocational model of ministry is strongly oriented toward the idea that the church is a means, not an end; that it is essentially incarnational, not essentially institutional. This means that building a model of a bivocational ministry means taking a clear set of positions in the conversation about ecclesiology. We will argue that an institutional understanding of the church has both led to, and resulted from, a firm-based approach to ecclesiology with the professionalized ministry at its center, one specific outcome of which is an essentially *transactional* understanding of what discipleship means. By contrast, an incarnational understanding of the church may point us toward, and be strengthened by, an understanding of the church that sees it as something operating more like a commons—one specific outcome of which is an essentially *relational* understanding of discipleship. This focus on authentic relationship is itself potentially the most dramatic and countercultural witness the Christian faith has to offer against the social forces arrayed against the message of the gospel.

Without becoming too deeply theological, in this chapter we'll chart out what all this means and explore the deeper vision of the church and its future from which a bivocational understanding of ministry springs.

5. Getting There from Here

One thing I know from spending a lifetime in the church is that we can be really good at describing and discussing ideas but not very good at translating these ideas into concrete proposals, creating a strategy to achieve our proposals, and measuring our progress toward them. Oftentimes we conclude with the idea that, if we just pray harder, the Holy Spirit will somehow come and do the work for us—or will somehow possess us to do it. I come to this work with the idea that what it means to be the body of Christ is that God is entrusting this work to us, and has already given us the hearts, the minds, and the strength sufficient for the task.

So we'll wrap up the book by setting out some specific proposals in each of the areas addressed by the previous chapters. I'll offer some ideas for how we can identify and raise up bivocational people to the ordained ministry; what changes distinguish a congregation that is moving toward a bivocational ethos, and how to measure progress toward those changes; and how larger denominational structures can examine their own basic assumptions with a view to opening space and possibility for the emergence of bivocational expressions of ministry.

After this Paul left Athens and went to Corinth. There he found a Jew named Aquila, a native of Pontus, who had recently come from Italy with his wife Priscilla, because Claudius had ordered all Jews to leave Rome. Paul went to see them, and, because he was of the same trade, he stayed with them, and they worked together—by trade they were tentmakers. Every Sabbath he would argue in the synagogue and would try to convince Jews and Greeks.

—Acts 18:1-4

Models of ministry have changed a lot since the days of the apostle Paul. One wonders what he would have made of all the trappings and affectations that have sprung up in the two millennia since he stitched tents together in the back alleys of Corinth to support his work with the nascent Christian community there, and his evangelism to communities outside the church.

Of course, the conditions of ministry were profoundly different then. Christianity was not the dominant cultural backdrop of the day. Most people had no idea of what was distinct or different about the Christian understanding of God and God's purposes, and those who did have some idea generally had a pretty bad, or at least misinformed, apprehension of it. Paul had to do the work of a disciple on the terms the culture gave him.

When we state it in these terms, however, it becomes quickly apparent that the parallels between Paul's day and our own may be closer and more numerous than we would at first imagine. Christianity is misunderstood in most places, and persecuted in more than a few. It has a complicated and often turbulent history that has caused many people to dismiss it as a source of moral authority. It is no longer the dominant force in places where it once held unchallenged cultural authority. And in many places matters of belief generally have become relegated to the private sphere, and made a matter limited to questions of individual conscience.

In these conditions, Paul's example has renewed force and salience. Tentmakers don't divide their existence between church on Sunday and the sewing floor on the weekdays. They are ministers *every* day, sometimes in church and sometimes in the world. They make community with other people who understand their own place in the faith community in similar terms. By coming together with each other, by making genuine community out of authentic relationships with each other, they receive the support and strength they need to do the work of disciples—which is, in the end, nothing more or less than to bring other people seeking relationship with the Source of all being into exactly that community of relationship. Mr. Smith, it turns out, was a tentmaker.

The tentmakers of Paul's day are the bivocational ministers of our day. All of them—all of *us*—are empowered in baptism to claim this ministry. Some of them become ordained. In the pages that follow, we'll look at how this works in a bivocational community, and how these communities offer a compelling and magnetic answer to the question of the future of the church in an increasingly secular society.

Chapter 1
The Bivocational Pastor

Mark Wastler gets up most mornings between 5:30 and 6:00. Before doing anything else, he pulls on his work clothes, heads out the kitchen door to the enclosed field behind his house, and checks on a flock of some seventy sheep. Wastler has lived on this farm for just under ten years. He tried a few ways to make it sustainable before settling on sheep farming. He can show you a spreadsheet in which he has carefully plotted out his costs for obtaining and feeding the lambs, the amount he projects the sheep will grow in weight, and the amount of profit he can expect to receive when the sheep go to market—assuming, that is, they all stay healthy and out of the clutches of the coyotes that range across his part of northwestern Virginia.

Sheep farming is a hard life. It makes for early mornings and, very often, late nights. When lambing season comes, sleep is a rare luxury. And notwithstanding the sweet image that most urban dwellers hold, sheep can be cantankerous, unpleasant, and clueless when it comes to keeping themselves out of danger. Come to think of it, that may be why for centuries the ordained leaders of congregations have been called pastors—a direct borrow of the Latin noun *pastor*, shepherd. People—at least people in the church—can be a lot like sheep.

In Wastler's case, the term turns out to be more than a little bit appropriate. Because he is also an ordained minister, and he serves as the rector—the senior (and in the case of his congregation, the only) ordained minister in an Episcopal church—in his parish. It's a parish seventy-three miles and two state boundaries away: Saint Paul's, in Sharpsburg, Maryland. It's a parish of some 170 or so members; on any given Sunday, about fifty-five of them are in church.

Mark Wastler is a bivocational pastor. So is Joseph Wilkes; he's the rector of Saint Andrew's in Methuen, Massachusetts, and an oral surgeon in Boston. So is Kate Harrigan; she's the rector of Saint Paul's Church and the chaplain at Saint Stephen's Episcopal School, both in Harrisburg, Pennsylvania. And so, as it turns out, are an increasing number of pastors across the mainline Protestant traditions.

Many pastors are part-time. More often than not, their status, as a wise mentor of mine once quipped, would more accurately be summarized as "partially compensated." They provide ordained leadership in the increasing number of faith communities that can only afford an ordained minister on a part-time basis; but the seeming limits on the time they give the parish are rarely rigidly observed, and the paradigm shaping how ministry is structured and shared between ordained and lay members of the community is still strongly shaped by the ideas and expectations of the "Standard Model" of ministry that takes for granted the presence of a full-time, benefitted professional in the clerical role. The expectations of the community, often based on an understanding of ordained ministry formed by decades of that model, as well as the discomfort that deters many pastors from insisting on the limits to their presence when there is work to be done, often make the idea of "part time" more of a semantic construction than a reality shaping the structure of ministry in a community.

But for bivocational pastors, those limits are very real. They exert strong grip on the whole parish, because they make it necessary for all members of the community—not just the pastor—to find different ways of sharing the responsibilities of ministry. Said plainly, the clear and unavoidable limits around the availability of bivocational pastors, the plain result of the restrictions placed on all of us with jobs in the secular world, requires the whole community, and not just its ordained leader, to come to terms with some basic questions about what ministry *is*. The good news is that, in a moment of tremendous change in the circumstances of the church, this confrontation with the meaning and structure of ministry may just be about the best thing we could ask for.

It's no longer the case that pastors like Mark Wastler, Joseph Wilkes, and Kate Harrigan are anomalies. As we will see in later chapters, the institution of the church may not yet be fully aware of, or fully responsive to, this bivocational reality; nonetheless, the weaving together of a number of economic, cultural, and societal forces have made it an adaptive response to a fundamentally changed set of circumstances.

The idea of ordained ministers of the church also working in a job outside the church is by no means new. On the contrary, it is very old indeed—just about as old as the church itself. In the eighteenth chapter of Acts, we find the apostle Paul in the midst of his second missionary journey, arriving in Corinth after leaving Athens. He ends up staying there for a year and a half, with Aquila and Priscilla, a married Jewish couple recently exiled from Rome. As Luke reports, "because he was of the same trade, he stayed with them, and they worked together—they were tentmakers" (Acts 18:3).

For many years it has been a commonplace to refer to ordained ministers working outside the church as people in a "tentmaking ministry," using the imagery of Paul's example. It is a tradition that has been expressed, in various ways, from the founding days of the church. Over the centuries of Christian history, the form and social structure of ordained ministry has taken on a variety of forms, ranging from monks in religious orders cloistered away from the secular world to Mennonite deacons working at a trade while pastoring their church. Each of these expressions, and countless more besides, are equally valid as expressions of a response to God's call to ordained ministry. The question that each must answer has to do with the gifts of the individual, the needs of the community, and the working of the Holy Spirit in a particular set of circumstances and within a particular gathering of the faithful. The instinct to define in narrow terms what ordained ministry should be, and then to make dogmatic significance of those contingent choices, is another example of our well-developed tendency to confuse the human instinct for creating systems of disposing power with God's relentless purpose to reconcile and restore humanity.

You may be reading this book because you're a member of a faith community—or maybe the leader of a faith community—on the cusp of having to make some hard decisions about the future structure of the ministry you offer. Or you may be reading this book because you're an ordained pastor thinking about taking on a pastorate in which you'd be spending some of your time in a job outside your role in the church.

In either case, there's one overarching reality to grapple with up front: the successful implementation of a bivocational model of ministry *is a work of the entire faith community*, and not just the ordained member (or members) of that community. "Bivocational ministry" is much more than a shorthand description of the working life of the pastor of a church. It's a way of describing a different way of thinking about how the ministry of the whole community works.

So at the outset, it's necessary to understand that much of the responsibility for the success of a bivocational model of ministry lies with the entire community; it's in the pews, not just in the pastor's study. Chapter 2 will deal more directly with the sorts of qualities that characterize congregations that make a success of bivocational ministry. Here, I want to focus first on the pastor. I do this *not* because all ministry begins with the pastor; all ministry begins with baptism, and with God's call to us in community. Instead, we'll begin with the pastor because, whether we like it or not, that is how our history, our institutions, our polity, and our organizational culture have taught us to think about ministry.

The Pastor in a Bivocational Community

What sort of pastor flourishes in the setting of bivocational ministry? Some of the qualities that contribute to success in this revisioned way of structuring the work of the faith community are obvious; some are less so. One thing is certain: The sort of person who tends to succeed in this reimagined expression of community ministry is in many ways quite distinct from the kind of person the coffee-hour ladies and the commissions on ministry have long thought would be "ideal" for the pastor's office.

Of course there's no one set of requirements for a pastor in bivocational ministry, just as there isn't for a pastor in the traditional "Standard Model." But there are some things to think about, if you're a person contemplating taking on such a role—a self-assessment that you might walk yourself through to come to a considered understanding of whether such a step might be a good expression of your gifts for ministry.

Let's group them into three categories: professional skills and interests, personal gifts and talents, and leadership style.

A. Your professional skills and circumstances

Professional skills. It may seem obvious, but bears stating plainly, that a precondition to success in bivocational ministry is a set of skills that equip you for work in the world outside the church. In practical terms this probably means that you have had a career of some sort *before* thinking about preparing for a role in the ordained ministry. Said differently, if your career path has been predominantly in an ordained role within the church, and you're now thinking of moving into some kind of role in which you'd also pick up another job alongside your work in ministry, your choices are likely to be fairly limited.

As the average age at ordination has increased across many denominations, the good news is that more and more people coming to the ordained ministry of the church bring with them professional accomplishments in the world outside the church. But those of us considering a bivocational path need to bring some holy scrutiny to our curriculum vitae. How current are our skills? How recent are our experiences?

Flexibility. A second consideration is the flexibility of your secular employment. The professional engagements among the bivocational clergy I surveyed in researching this book were tremendously varied, but the clear theme in all of them was a fair degree of latitude in setting one's own schedule. Pastoral needs, like the hospitalization or death of a member of the community, do not neatly schedule themselves around other professional demands.

Of course, there are two dimensions to this flexibility. One is the willingness of a cleric's employer outside the church to be understanding when an unexpected absence arises. The other, which we'll explore more fully in the next chapter, is the flexibility of the parish itself in adapting its expectations around the pastoral presence of the ordained minister, whether that means lifting up a stronger pastoral visitation ministry of the laity, or (as seems more frequently the case) finding comfort with the practice of holding funerals or memorial services on evenings or weekends, when more people are likely to be able to take part anyway.

A couple of points are worth considering here. It might seem as though the ordained minister in a self-employed position outside the church—a sheep-farmer, like Mark Wastler, or an oral surgeon, or a realtor, or a therapist, or a software coder—might have the greatest degree of flexibility. It turns out that this is not necessarily the case, as any self-employed person will quickly tell you. Any form of work that is client-focused—even if the clients are lambs—needs to be responsive to the needs of clients, and conflicts will inevitably arise between those demands and the expectations of the faith community for the presence of its pastor. The single most important aspect of managing those conflicts is not to find ways of avoiding them; they can't be avoided. Rather, it's to anticipate them, discussing together as a faith community how everyone together will handle them—rather than dealing with them as they arise.

Integration. One other consideration in a self-assessment for bivocational ministry is a reflection on how, and how naturally, you feel the ideas and insights of one area of your professional life integrate with your work in the ministry of the church (and vice-versa). This turns out to be crucially important, for a number of reasons.

First, and perhaps most important, your own spiritual health depends on how well you can integrate these two aspects of your working life. If your work outside the church is in a setting in which your organization's goals conflict with the ethical claims of your faith—and you feel unable to articulate that conflict in ways that will be heard—you'll quickly become less effective in both spheres. Less obvious, but equally as difficult, are circumstances in which your workplace outside the church has an organizational culture indifferent or even hostile toward the influence of religious belief in shaping choices about life priorities. Many workplaces set out policies of neutrality toward, or acceptance of, all faiths in the workplace, but then actively promote a working culture that effectively creates conflict between success in the organization and the choices we make to devote time, the only finite resource, to our spiritual lives.

Still, there's a profound gift in this conundrum for the ordained minister in a bivocational role. It's simply this: it places us in *exactly* the same circumstances that every other member of our faith community already confronts in their own working lives, and by doing so places us alongside our people in living out our shared call to Christian ministry. It gives us deeper familiarity with the pressures every Christian in the post-industrial twenty-first-century economy has to make, and through that familiarity gives us greater credibility as leaders in those communities, helping people to navigate those choices. This is a source of *informal* authority, as contrasted with the sort of *formal* authority that hierarchy confers; we'll take up this distinction more deeply in chapter 3.

Here's one example. At one point in my own work in ministry, it became clear that the job I held outside the church—a grant-funded job in higher education—was likely coming to an end. When it became evident that I would need to be focusing time and energy into a search for a new position, I spoke to members of the parish vestry—the governing body of the congregation—and, eventually, to many members of the parish. It was a moment of considerable stress; my work outside the church provided not just a salary but health insurance for my family, and the possibility of investing in a retirement plan. Eventually a new job came along, and what had loomed as a transition that would bring some hard decisions instead brought some new commuting patterns, and not much else in the way of change.

The real lesson of this experience came later that year—at stewardship time. I gave what I regarded as a middling sermon on Stewardship Sunday, and as the service ended I found myself walking into coffee hour thinking of all the things I wished I'd said. My epiphany came when another member of the parish—a man about my age working in the private sector—approached me privately and gave me a compliment I didn't feel I deserved. But then he explained it: "You know, somehow it was different this year, listening to you. I knew—we all knew—you had a hard moment there about the job. A lot of us have been there. I don't know, maybe it made it easier to believe you or something. I get it that you have to earn a paycheck just like I do."

I still think about that conversation. It had never occurred to me, in the years I worked full-time in (and only in) ministry, that when I stood in a pulpit and presumed to speak about the economics of stewardship, or the way we all share in carrying out the financial responsibilities of the parish, that at least some folks were having a hard time taking me seriously. From their perspective, my family didn't experience anything like the economic risk they faced every day. Even the most accomplished and well-compensated members of a parish can experience sudden and precipitous reversals; living with that knowledge can make people understandably risk-averse when it comes to judging how much they should commit in their annual gift to the parish.

At least for that member of my parish—and, I now realize, many more besides—a full-time minister didn't have any way of understanding the way their economic lives had to be lived. But that changed, significantly, when my own principal source of income and access to benefits became a job outside the church—a job with all the ups and downs, all the vicissitudes and all the risks, of the jobs people hold in the pews of our church.

Second, your sense of flourishing as an ordained member of the community working in a role outside the church will likely be directly related to your ability to find and share insights from one part of your working life in the other. One of the most thoughtful examples I've met of this ability lived out is Elliot Moss, who is the vicar of Saint John's Church, an Episcopal church in the town of Ashfield, one of the "hill towns" of western Massachusetts. Elliot also expanded my understanding of the range of jobs bivocational pastors do; he's a tenured professor of computer science at the University of Massachusetts at Amherst.

I wasn't surprised when the ministers I met researching this book worked as teachers, counselors, non-profit executives, or even in healing professions like nurses and oral surgeons. But computer scientists?

When we sat down for coffee, Elliot did his best to explain in terms I could grasp what he does in his academic research. "Really, what I study is systems," he summarized, "and systems work or don't work for specific reasons. So when I came to Saint John's, I tried to think of the community in terms of systems—what systems worked? Which ones didn't? What did the working systems have to teach us about fixing or rebuilding the systems that weren't working?"

My own experience has a parallel to Elliot's. When I was called to my first genuinely bivocational post in ministry, my work in the secular world was running a cross-disciplinary behavioral science laboratory in a university. The people who were my colleagues in that setting were social psychologists, behavioral economists, and a range of other scholars exploring the peculiar ways in which our decisions are made. Our lab provided a facility for researchers to conduct experiments, and to monitor things like heart rate, blood pressure, and hormone levels in the people who were answering the questions the researchers had designed.

While the connection might not be evident at first (or even second) glance, the more I spoke with these investigators about their findings the clearer it became to me how I might apply their insights in the life of the parish. Many of them studied how our decisions are often not merely mechanistic, rational calculations, but processes of choice shaped unconsciously but predictably by our emotional lives. And in some cases, our emotional makeup seems to be aligned with the way we set our priorities in the moral sphere. People who tend to be angry are most animated around issues of rights and freedoms, for example, while people who tend to rise quickly to a feeling of disgust are likely to place great value in ideas of purity.[4]

A community of faith is, among many other blessings, a community of people striving to live their lives in terms of their moral aspirations.

---

4. Dacher Keltner, E. J. Horberg, and Christopher Oveis, "Emotions as Moral Intuitions," in Joseph P. Forgas, ed., *Affect in Social Thinking and Behavior* (London: Psychology Press, 2006), 165.

Of course, those aspirations don't always align, much less harmonize. I realized that the parish I'd been called to had just endured a pretty difficult period of loss and disappointment, and that this shared emotion was shaping how the people in it understood the possibilities ahead and the priorities we should seek. Because of my work outside the church, I knew there were resources within the community of scientists who study these things that could give me some insights about how to acknowledge this—and help the community move forward toward a better, healthier place.

Most bivocational pastors know the feeling of being identified in their secular workplace as a counselor, mentor, or sounding board. What seems to help people flourish in this role is the ability to bring insights from each world into the other—to see a parish in terms of its systems, for example, like Elliot Moss. So if this is a form of ministry you see yourself offering, it will be worth taking a moment to ask: what tools do I have from the work I've done outside the church that can strengthen the gifts I bring to the church's ministry?

B. Your Personal Gifts and Needs

There is a broad variety of gifts that find expression in ordained ministry. There is also—let's be honest here— an equally broad range of needs that draw people into the ordained ministry of the church.

My first boss in ministry taught me this lesson in a way I'll never forget. Not long after new seminarians signed on for a fieldwork rotation in the place I first served—which happened to be in a large, nondenominational university church with a large staff—the senior pastor brought us in, sat us down, and early in the conversation asked a simple question: "Why do you think you want to be ordained?"

After you'd stammered through the answer you had likely already practiced on your parish discernment committee or congregational support group, and had deployed in your interviews with the Commission on Ministry, he smiled kindly and said, "What you've shared with me is why you think you *should* be ordained. But what I asked you was why you *want* to be—what's in it for you. Have you thought about that?"

I'm not sure what answer my colleagues in the seminarian corps offered to this question. I'll admit that, when it came my turn for that conversation, the question stopped me cold. To that point I'd genuinely never considered it. What's more, I wasn't at all sure it was a question I was *allowed* to consider.

When my blushing face signaled my inability to respond, my boss offered me this bit of wisdom: "Nearly everyone who offers themselves to an ordination process is looking for something. They're looking for the attention, or for the respect, or for the love they didn't receive as a child. It doesn't really matter what it is you're looking for. But it *does* matter that you figure out what you're looking for—or else it will lead you around by the nose."

I left the office more than a little abashed. But in the nearly twenty years that have passed since that day, I've come to appreciate the wisdom of my boss's insight. I'm an only child, and my family was, to say it generously, a little complicated growing up. Having the respect of my community was something I craved, in a way that was both deep and largely unconscious. Growing up in the church, and observing the regard paid to the ordained leader of that community, made a considerable impact on me.

Some of the personal needs we bring to our work in ordained ministry align well with work in a bivocational setting. And some, to be very candid, don't. No matter how you approach the prospect of working in a bivocational pastorate—whether you're a full-time pastor thinking of moving in this direction, or a person considering ordination to offer ordained ministry alongside the work you do already—it will serve you well to spend some time in prayerful reflection about your own needs in ordained work.

If you have a need to be the center of the faith community you're a part of—to be the designer, chief architect, and principal spokesperson of the community's goals in carrying out the ministry of the church—a bivocational parish probably won't be a happy place for you. And if one of the things you seek in being ordained is a sense of distinction and differentiation from the lay members of the congregation, it's not likely that this style of ministry will be fulfilling to you. One trait I found in common among practically all of the bivocational ministers I've been privileged to meet—at least those who flourish in the role—is a willingness to interrogate everything that creates a distinction between ordained and lay ministries, to evaluate them against the standards of necessity and efficacy, and to give up those distinctions that have come more from custom than from scriptural evidence or theological ground.

Much the same goes for authority. Being an ordained minister within a Christian community confers a degree of authority. The French philosopher Michel Foucault held the view that while a relationship between a pastor and a flock was a central metaphor for leadership in a variety of ancient cultures, in Christianity it took on a kind of authority that made it a core idea for the authority of state power in the development of Western culture.[5] But the exercise of that authority can take many different forms, expressed in both formal and informal ways. Pastors successful in bivocational settings tend to have less interest in *formal* sources of authority— the structures that create the distinctions noted above—while being adept at understanding how *informal* authority works in the context of their specific communities. They look for ways to hand over formal authority in meaningful and observable ways, while finding ways of exercising informal authority in more subtle ways.

If you are more comfortable with roles that come with a relatively high degree of formal authority, or if you find that is what attracts you

---

5. Michel Foucault, "Pastoral power and political reason," in *Religion and Culture: Michel Foucault*, ed. and trans. Jeremy R. Carrette (New York: Routledge, 1999), 135-152.

to the work that you do, bivocational ministry probably won't be a place of great satisfaction for you. By contrast, if you sense in yourself a need for social engagement and inclusion, this style of ministry will answer those needs in rich and varied ways. The work of ordained ministry has places for a pretty wide range of introverts and extroverts, but—at least in the observations I've made of these parishes—folks who tend toward the naturally extroverted seem to be better aligned with the challenges of a bivocational pastorate.

And if you sense in yourself a need for the deep connections of genuine community, a place in a gathering of faithful people who live out their call to love each other even when *liking* each other is not always easy, then a bivocational setting might be a place that brings out your gifts for ministry in rich and rewarding ways.

Everyone who takes part in the life of a faith community comes with an offer to make—an offer of gifts, of skills, of talents, of energy, of interests. Too often our understanding of ministry *in* the church has focused on the gifts and skills of the pastor alone. (Think of it this way: Why do some churches put the name of the pastor on the sign outdoors? What is it meant to communicate? What does it say about that community's understanding of ministry?) Not all people in ministry have the same interest, desire, or skill around developing the gifts of others. There is nothing wrong or surprising about that. Not all virtuoso performers are good teachers, and not all great teachers are excellent soloists. Bivocational pastors—at least those who are happy and who tend to flourish in the role—are more likely to be teachers than virtuoso soloists. They would rather lead from within the ensemble, playing along with the same music, than be the featured performer playing a solo in front. But that gets us to the last consideration: the way you most naturally exercise leadership.

C. Your Leadership Style

Just as there are a variety of gifts that people bring to ordained ministry, there are a variety of leadership styles that can make for successful work in congregational life. Success in a bivocational pastorate, however, seems to be associated with a pretty specific list of leadership styles. That means it's probably a pretty good idea to ask yourself, as you approach the possibility of such a role, whether your own style of leadership will make for a good match.

At the risk of stating the obvious, let's begin with a simple assertion: ordained ministry is a ministry of leadership. This would not, at first glance, seem a controversial statement, if only because in the Standard Model of ministry there are a number of assumptions about roles the ordained minister will perform within, and for the benefit of, the larger community—roles beyond the one-on-one role of pastoral counseling, or even beyond public role of presiding over the worship offered by the community. And yet, leadership is not itself traditionally an area of focus of the training offered in seminaries, and the capacity for leadership is not generally a factor systematically considered by commissions on ministry in identifying those called to ordained ministry.

Over the past century—since the emergence of the study of management as a clear academic discipline—a vast literature has emerged on leadership. It is not possible here to survey all of the theories, findings, and methodologies of that literature, but two basic observations can help orient a study of leadership as it applies to a specific pastor in a specific context of congregational life.

The first of these is that all of us in leadership positions have a sense of how we function as leaders. That is to say, we have a sense of our own leadership style. The second of these—as true as the first—is that our communities also have a sense of our leadership style, a perception often different from our own. A first question to ask, then, has to do with how closely aligned these two perspectives are. Are you seen by others in the congregation in much the same way you see yourself? Or do these two perspectives diverge? If they do, in what ways? To find the answer to these questions, you first need to be able to find and accept candid input from members of the community. Once you've done this, ask yourself how much work you are willing to do, as an ordained minister, to listen to and learn from your community—about what's most and least effective about your exercise of leadership, to understand how you are perceived, and to consider how that perception may differ from how you imagine yourself.

Success in any form of leadership—but especially in the kind of community in which a bivocational pastorate takes root—is significantly conditioned by the presence of this alignment. To draw on two well-studied archetypes at opposite poles of a spectrum, if you see yourself as a laissez-faire sort of leader, allowing those in the community to pursue their own interests and develop their own skills, but are perceived as micromanager, providing direction and controlling developments at a close level, then there's a good chance your efforts to exercise leadership will be misunderstood and limited in their impact. If you see yourself as an effective delegator, but are perceived as distant and distracted, you may well have difficulty finding the ground under your feet in a faith community that will depend on the effective and coordinated sharing of responsibility.

While there is a place within ordained ministry for a wide range of leadership styles, that is somewhat less the case in the particular circumstances of bivocational ministry. Because success in a bivocational pastorate is connected in deep ways to the encouragement and unleashing of the ministerial gifts of all members of the congregation, effective leadership in this setting depends on skills centered in interpersonal connection, clarity of communication, and comfort with leading from the side rather than the front. To use an image familiar to readers of leadership scholar

Ronald Heifitz, successful leadership in a bivocational pastorate takes someone who knows when it's necessary to go up to the balcony to see the whole dance floor, and who also knows when it's time to come down and dance on it along with everyone else.[6]

In my visits with faith communities living out a bivocational pastorate, I observed one consistent leadership skill that distinguished ordained ministers thriving in the role: the ability to get others to say "yes." There are a lot of ways of describing this skill—empowering the laity, lifting up the skills and gifts of all members of the community, mutual ministry— but no matter how it's labeled, it boils down to being able to get others to step up and take their part in the shared work of ministry.

The bad news is, many of us who come into the ministry are the sort of folks who are easy to say "no" to. There are good reasons for that. We don't want to appear judgmental. We don't want to be demanding. We want to be pastorally sensitive to the many burdens carried by all members of the community. And we're forgiving, because we're in the forgiveness business. So it becomes easier to do the thing ourselves instead of asking for help—printing the Sunday bulletin, getting the food offerings to the pantry, organizing the scripture readers, running the bible study, you name it. And we may even do it well—but that doesn't help the community grow into healthy patterns of shared ministry in the long run.

The good news is, becoming the sort of leader who can get people to say "yes" is only about ten percent charisma and ninety percent learned skill. The first step is something we just covered—a willingness to do some work understanding how you are perceived by the community as a leader among other leaders. The second step is doing the work of exploring and learning about what motivates each member of the community to be part of the community's work. One consideration is critical: the reasons

---

6. Ronald Heifetz, *Leadership Without Easy Answers* (Cambridge, Mass.: The Belknap Press of Harvard University Press, 1994), 252–24.

that you went into the ministry are almost certainly not the reasons why the members of your community come to church. Think of it this way: for most of us who went into ministry, our love of the liturgy and the life of worship means that there's almost no problem we can't imagine solving by laying on another worship service. But in the life of small parishes, that is the sort of answer that can quickly sap the community of energy by spreading the glowing embers of the fire too thin.

The final step is connecting in a clear way each person's motivations with the needs of the community's ministry, less by asking than by helping them see the connection themselves. Sometimes what this requires is not so much a skillful recruitment pitch, but rather work on the task of making the community's *needs* clearer. I'm surprised how often simply taking the time to explain, for example, what eucharistic ministers are and why they are important to the whole life of the community somehow seems to flush out volunteers who would never have agreed to a flat-out request from me to sign up.

This much is certainly true: Leadership in a bivocational pastorate is a great way to learn more about yourself, and the way you are seen in your community. Those lessons are sometimes deeply affirming, and sometimes deeply humbling. If you can keep the prayerful discipline of being open to both of those possibilities, chances are you will find this a place in which you can thrive.

Leadership is an inherently social work. There is no meaningful concept of leadership separated from the life of a human community. Exactly because of this, there is one final and increasingly significant consideration to bear in mind—one on which both individual pastors and faith communities need to reflect. It is simply that how we see ourselves as leaders, and how we are seen as leaders, is not only a product of our own skills and how they are expressed; it is something deeply conditioned by social expectations and often invisible cultural narratives.

I am fortunate enough to be of an age that I knew members of the first generation of women who were ordained in my church. Those pioneers found themselves having to confront in every moment of their vocation a set of cultural expectations deeply ingrained in both church and society that said women could not possibly be leaders—at least not of faith communities. Not only did they have to challenge those expectations directly; they had to teach, and to demonstrate, that what "leadership" meant in the context of congregations could be something broader than the notions we had received from centuries of our cultural inheritance.

That work is still going on. So too is the work of imagining that leadership can be exercised by people of color, by people of all sexual orientations (and none), by the differently abled and socioeconomically underprivileged. Each pastor contemplating the idea of entering into a bivocational pastorate needs to reflect prayerfully on how these dynamics might play out in the specific context of a given congregation. Theologically and theoretically we want to be committed to the notion that anyone, of any background and any orientation, can lead any community anywhere; but the practical reality is that leadership is highly contextual, and an individual pastor who might thrive in one setting might well stumble in another—even one that, to all outward appearances (size, setting, demographic composition) appeared to be nearly the same.

To say all this is simply to acknowledge that leadership is an expression of authority—and the exercise of authority in community always happens in both formal and informal ways. We'll look in more depth at these two categories in chapter 3; here, our focus is on the individual pastor. In a bivocational pastorate, that individual needs to be alert to how the unique circumstances of their own gender, race, age, sexual orientation, education, socioeconomic status, and other considerations have had an impact on *their own* understanding of their capabilities as a leader—how they have conditioned it, and perhaps caused either an over- or under-estimating tendency to shape their self-understanding. And as though this weren't enough, the individual pastor needs to be sensitive to how the unique personality of the congregation—an idea we turn to next—translates the cues of these categories of identity into an assessment of leadership ability.

As Christians, our identity is ultimately rooted in the risen Christ. Yet as Christians living in the early twenty-first century, and as pastors exercising a ministry of leadership, it is for us to prayerfully reflect on, and skillfully act on, how the very real interplay of identity and stereotype condition the ways we offer our gifts to the work of the church.

Chapter 2
The Bivocational Congregation

Saint Luke's in Hastings, Minnesota had come to a crossroads. A major project to improve access to the building for the disabled had taken a significant share of the endowment—and caused a rift in the congregation. Many chose to leave. Dollars left with them. Quickly, the reality became apparent to the congregation's leaders: they could no longer afford a full-time rector. Difficult conversations followed. The rector, who had been among the first to see the writing on the wall, was—happily for the congregation—able to accept a change in her status in order to stabilize the parish's finances. But a short-term fix could not be a long-term solution. Made aware of the parish's circumstances, the head of the judiciary—in this case, the bishop of the Episcopal Church in Minnesota—became involved.

James Jelinek, then the Bishop of Minnesota, had seen stories like Saint Luke's before, and those experiences shaped his response to their circumstances. After visiting the parish and meeting with its leaders, he gave the community two options. They could decide to prepare the affairs of the parish for an orderly closure. Said differently, they could give up. Or they could reimagine how church was done. They would start by undertaking a survey of the entire membership of the parish, asking each member to identify their gifts for contributing to the ministry of the parish—their talents, their gifts, their skills, and yes, their financial ability to contribute. They would compile the findings of that survey and decide if the resources existed for them to carry on. If they chose that path, they would identify a team of leaders from among themselves—all lay people—to share the necessary work of a faith community: the administration, the property, the Christian education, the pastoral outreach, the mission and service to the world outside the church. And oh, yes, the worship. Two of the members of that leadership team, the bishop explained, would be held up by the whole community as the right people to provide sacramental ministry. And they would be *ordained* by the bishop. Then, while doing their work in the world and serving the church as ordained ministers, they would also be required to take part in a series of courses at the diocese's School of Formation.

It was a tall order. Some members of the parish didn't think they could do it. Others were perplexed at the idea of ordaining someone they might *know*. Someone sitting right next to them in the pews. Sure, there were natural leaders in the congregation—there are in every congregation. But ordain them?

In the end, that is what the parish chose to do. When I visited them, they had been living into their new model of ministry for nearly ten years. The two members of the ministry team who had been ordained—one a contractor, the other a civil engineer—had served alongside the previous rector during a two-year transition period; after that, they had been on their own in providing for the ordained needs of the community. As I met with them after church one Sunday, I was introduced to members of the new ministry team, members of the parish who had just begun to step into their duties as the successor generation of that first group of ministry leaders. Two of them, through a process of discernment, had been identified as the next ordained leaders of the community and had already begun to prepare for their ordinations.

❖

Congregations are as different as the people in them, and certainly as different as the people who lead them. Those differences are in part a function of size, as Arlin Rothauge noted in his now-classic pamphlet *Sizing Up a Congregation For New Member Ministry.*[7] Rothauge's insight was that congregational *size* tends to shape the *style* of communication and collaboration within faith communities—and, in consequence, the role of, and expectations focused on, the senior pastor in these communities.

Anyone who has experienced more than one church along their journey can testify that each faith community—just like each workplace, or each neighborhood, or each school—has a unique personality. We often say that different groups have a different "feel" to them. What we mean is that the community, as a group of people gathered for a purpose, have an agreed (if not always explicit) sense of what matters and what does not, how things are done and why they are done that way, and what sort of contributions to the community's work and witness are most welcome— and which are not.

The personalities of congregations are varied, despite the fact that virtually every congregation would describe itself, first and foremost, as "welcoming." What we usually mean by that word, even if we don't realize it, is something more like, "We're really welcoming to folks who can figure out pretty quickly how we work and what we care about, and who find themselves comfortable in that kind of place." While every congregation should strive to be as welcoming as possible, congregations are made up of humans—and humans have limits, one of which is a tendency to gather into groups of people who quickly realize, and find assurance in, their similarities. Not every congregation is for everyone. Sometimes

---

7. Arlin Rothauge, *Sizing Up a Congregation for New Member Ministry* (New York: Episcopal Church Center, 1983).

what makes for the fit, or lack of it, is the way in which the community understands, shapes, and responds to the role of its ordained minister.

Of course, congregations were not created by God to always and forever be at a specific size. Congregations grow and shrink, as do the neighborhoods around them, the ministries to which they are called, and the resources at their disposal. The identity of a parish, its ethos and ways of doing things, can be deeply shaped by years of ministry at one general size and shape—and then find itself challenged when a change in circumstances makes a transition inevitable.

Alice Mann, in her book *Raising the Roof: The Pastoral to Program-Sized Transition*, focused her research on the second and third of Rothauge's categories of congregational size. She looked in particular at the idea that congregations were striving to grow *larger*, and were encountering difficulties in shifting from the structure and communication patterns of one size to those more appropriate to the other.[8] But congregations don't always change by growing larger. Sometimes they "grow smaller," a seemingly nonsensical but increasingly meaningful idea. It is true that the difficulties facing some faith communities are overwhelming, and that sometimes the inevitability of closure can only be staved off by selling off the family silver (or spending down the parish endowment). But it is not true that all congregations that become smaller are destined for trouble. Some of them become stronger, deeper, more centered on the message of the gospel, and more intentional in their ministry to the world beyond the church as they contend with shifts in demographics and dollars. Getting to that outcome is not (or not merely) a matter of God's grace; it is a task for leadership, and the result of both prayer and planning.

In short, some congregations are better positioned to "grow smaller" than others. In my research visits to a number of congregations, I found

8. Alice Mann, *Raising the Roof: The Pastoral-to-Program Size Transition* (Bethesda, Md.: Alban Institute / Rowman and Littlefield, 2001).

a wide variety of models of ministry, but a fairly consistent set of themes about what separates those able to adapt from those that cannot. Of course, not all congregations successfully responding to changes in their circumstances adopt a bivocational approach to ministry; there are other ways of structuring ministry, and other possibilities for moving toward a future very different from our past. In what follows, I'll focus on what I observed to be consistent among congregations that have not only shifted into a bivocational approach to ministry, but that have found in it a source of growth and renewal.

The Place of the Pastor

Just as there are many different kinds of congregations—in terms of size, demography, spiritual gifts, and "community personality"—so there is considerable variety in the role of the pastor within the congregation. And, just as, in chapter 1, we explored the needs of individual *pastors* in expressing their gifts for ministry in an ordained role, it's equally true that the *congregation* has needs—and expectations—about what its role will be in the relationship between pastor and parish.

In *Raising the Roof,* Mann offers an interesting broad-brush insight into the relationship between the size of a congregation and the relative emphasis that congregation is likely to place on the person and the gifts of the pastor—or, alternatively, on the gifts of those within the laity. She describes an "N-curve" (figure 1) that shows an expected direction of growth, and with it a key aspect of changes in expectations, roles, and patterns of collaboration in the ministry of a community. But growth in the church never happens in one direction—and certainly is not happening that way today. As congregations "grow smaller" (something very different from "shrinking"), Mann's N-Curve takes on something of a different shape—which we can represent with the slightly modified form of her original idea, shown in figure 2.

FIGURE I: SIZE TRANSITION "N-CURVE," AFTER MANN

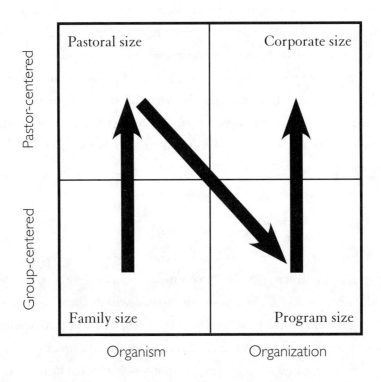

What Mann's insight reveals is that the role of the pastor is different in different types of congregations, and, therefore, so are the skills and gifts across the whole congregation on which flourishing depends. Taking this line of thinking one step further, the suggestion of Mann's analysis is that congregations that are relatively more "group centered" than "pastor centered" will likely find themselves better suited to a bivocational pastorate, exactly because the ethos of such congregations already accords a high degree of autonomy to, and depends for much of its energy on, the initiative of its lay members.

Going on just the examples of the parishes I visited in researching this book—admittedly a limited sample—that hypothesis is borne out

FIGURE 2: AN UPDATED "N-CURVE"

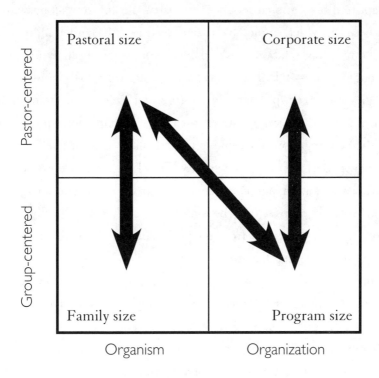

in experience. And there is an irony here, one important to consider at some length.

You might think that there is a simple, linear relationship between congregational size and the need for, and openness to, a bivocational pastorate. The idea would go something like this: the bigger the congregation, the less disposed and the less suited it will be to a bivocational structure for its ministry; the smaller the congregation, the more open and prepared it will be for experimenting with such a structure. That intuitive judgment seems to fit well with the needs of parishes, because the bigger the church, the less apparent need there is for changing the basic structure of how ministry is done.

But that turns out *not* to be the case. The ability of a congregation to adapt to a bivocational model of ministry and to grow along with it is not necessarily determined by its size. Instead, it has much more to do with the way that relationships and expectations have been expressed in that congregation—whether it has been "group centered" (family sized or program sized) or "pastor centered" (pastoral sized or corporate sized).

Group-centered congregations turn out, perhaps not surprisingly, to be the congregations most likely to find that a bivocational ministry offers new paths for growth and vitality. They have a community ethos of openness, affirmation, and engagement toward the gifts and energies of individuals and groups within the community, and, most critically, do not chiefly derive their identity from the person of the pastor.[9] We'll explore this in a little more depth in a later section.

This observation opens a few interesting and counterintuitive paths toward the future—at least for some congregations. To stick with Rothauge's categories for a moment, if group-centered congregations are most likely to succeed in adapting to a bivocational ethos of ministry, then two kinds of congergations—very small, family-sized faith communities (the "less-than-fifty-active-member" churches), and rather larger, 150- to 350-active-member program-sized churches—are likely to be the best candidates for making a successful transition to this approach. It's worth restating here a point made earlier, and one that will come up again: A

---

9. In the previous chapter I mentioned in passing the curious practice of outdoor signs. Strange though it may seem, I found this single piece of hardware to be a fairly telling (if simple) indicator of whether a parish would easily adapt to a bivocational pastorate. In none of the parishes I visited that were thriving in this style of ministry was the pastor's name (or the names of the ordained members of the ministry team) included on the outdoor sign—e.g., "The Rev. John Doe Smith, Rector." This is a custom rarely seen on signs outside Roman Catholic or Orthodox churches; it seems to be a practice peculiar to churches in the Protestant family. But its presence does seem to telegraph the way in which the community gathered inside the building understands the place and role of the senior ordained member, and how it defines its identity with reference to that person.

bivocational ministry is *a work of the entire congregation*; it is not merely a way of describing the working life of one person who happens to be ordained. It's a ministry in which an ordained minister (1) lives out the life of ministry with jobs both in the church and in the secular world, (2) models a way of living into the ministry of the baptized *both inside and outside the church* in a way that helps all members of the community to do the same, in ways appropriate to their circumstances, and (3) shares both the responsibility *and the authority* of aspects of the shared ministry of the community with lay members of the community. It turns out that the right place from which to do these things need not be, and ideally will not be, in the very center of the social structure of the congregation, the typical focal point at which the pastor is situated.

It may seem odd to place pastors of larger parishes in the category of those who might succeed in a bivocational pastorate. Don't the pastors of large congregations have quite enough on their plate just attending to the demands of parish ministry? A moment's reflection on the question suggests a different picture. In larger congregations, the resources often exist for two or three ordained ministers to be on the staff. In these settings, the senior pastor often is deeply engaged in community leadership in ways outside the life of the church—serving on boards, starting non-profits doing work aligned with the ministry goals of the parish, or perhaps teaching in a local setting of higher education. Exactly because these parishes are so well-resourced, part of the ministry exercised by the ordained leadership can be outside the church in ways that, very similar to pastors in poorly-resourced churches, help to make their perspectives on the life of discipleship more relevant to the experience of people in the pews.

So it is by no means only small, economically precarious churches that might find the bivocational model of ministry both attractive and a source of spiritual growth. In fact, success in a congregation's embracing and flourishing in a bivocational pastorate is not really—or at least not primarily—a matter of resources. Instead, what seems to be the critical element on which bivocational models of ministry is built is the presence of a group-centered ethos in the congregation. What does that look like in practice?

Moving Places

When I first came as the ordained leader to Saint John's in Newtonville, the parish had searched for a new full-time rector only just a few months before. They had issued a call in great hope to someone who, before ever appearing on the scene, made it clear to the parish and the bishop that he was not yet ready to handle responsibly the pastoral confidences that come with being the senior pastor of a congregation. The parish had found itself in the painful position of withdrawing its call, knowing that the fundamental bond of trust upon which all successful ministry is built could not be restored.

Blessings sometimes come disguised as disasters. What the parish realized, as they sat with the pieces of a broken search process all around them, was that the longstanding tradition of that parish to have a full-time, fully benefited senior pastor had driven them to look for someone who would simply repeat the pattern, without really considering an alternative. But the disappointing end of the search brought a new clarity in considering the financial realities of the parish. There was no way to afford that model of ministry anymore, given the costs of that one full-time professional and the other costs associated with maintaining a small non-profit organization with its own building and grounds in eastern Massachusetts.

Describing new ways of sharing the work of that ministry between a new pastor (who turned out to be me) and the members of the congregation turned out to be the easy part. We drafted a contract, had it reviewed by the usual authorities in our judicatory, and went to work. The harder part was changing the culture, one that had grown up around the expectation of a full-time pastor: a person who was pretty much always available, who decided on everything from the hymns on Sunday and the themes in sermons to the kind of paper purchased for the office, and who represented the church in its dealings with everyone from the trash haulers to the landscapers.

Two simple questions turned out to be the most powerful tools available to us in helping us understand how that old culture worked and how we might change it. The questions were "What do you expect the pastor to do?" and "How necessary is it for a pastor to do that?"

At first we tried this simply as an exercise of posing these two questions in the abstract. But as time went on, we walked ourselves through a variety of imagined scenarios. What if someone comes through the door asking for a handout? What if the child of someone who was married in the church sixty years ago appears on the doorstep asking whether we can host a funeral for a parent who has just died? What if the alarm system goes off in the middle of the day when the nursery school is in session downstairs?

Asking questions like this, and dozens more like them, became a low-risk but powerful means of bringing to the surface a whole set of expectations that old culture had inculcated in us about what pastors *should* be and what they *should* do. And asking them in ways safely separated—at least initially—from actual cases in our lives together helped us find ways to question those assumptions, discern anew what was central to the call to ordained ministry, and reimagine how other necessary aspects of the community's work might be done. Rather than a moment of crisis causing unexpected pain and misunderstanding as we adjusted to new ways of being a church together, we imagined those new ways as we thought through different scenarios. Eventually a picture of the more mutual sharing of responsibility and authority began to appear more clearly, and, as it did, people began to see new ways in which they could take up parts of the work of the community—because they found ways of becoming more deeply connected to their love of their community and the people in it.

The moment I knew Saint John's had become a place with a different culture and a different spirit didn't happen in a particularly celebratory way. It was four years after I'd begun my service as the pastor of the parish when, instead of being on a scheduled flight to return home after a business trip, I found myself flat on my back in a hospital bed a thousand miles from the church—on a Saturday. I'd presented myself to the emergency room not having the slightest idea why I had a seizing pain in my left flank. It turned out I had managed to assemble an impressive collection of kidney stones, which were building up a kidney infection behind them at a very fast rate. When I finally got my head around the fact that I wasn't going to leave the hospital that day, I let the leaders of the parish know. I offered to do what I could to find a substitute.

"It's okay," came the answer. "Don't worry. Just get better. We got this."

And, wouldn't you just know it, they really *did*. I learned the oddly liberating lesson that the whole life of the parish—even its worship life, that thing at the center of any faith community—didn't depend entirely on me.

Life for the Pastor in a Group-Centered Congregation

What had happened in those four intervening years is that the culture of Saint John's had shifted away from a long, deep history of being focused on the pastor toward something more about the community itself—centered, that is, on the people, rather than on the one person in a collar. I wish I could say this shift happened as the result of a clear strategy and a series of conscious, calculated steps. But it didn't.

Instead, it happened because of the happy combination of a number of forces. It happened because the shift from a full-time to a part-time minister allowed the congregation to reassess its financial priorities and invest in things that had long been chronically underfunded. It happened because, in ways large and small, we all worked on asking ourselves what was really necessary about the ordained ministry within the community. Some things about that role were necessary, to be sure, but much less than we had all been raised to think. And it happened because people began to step into roles that they felt they could take on, or to try volunteer commitments they thought they might be able to handle—at first a few, and then more.

If you are a close reader of the works I've cited above, a thought may be occurring to you. Think back to a moment to figure 1. In describing the four sizes of congregation, Alice Mann also divides them into two groups: those that are more *group*-centered (family sized and program sized), and those that are more *pastor*-centered (pastoral sized and corporate sized). My point is that it is not a linear progression from pastor- to group-centered. The smallest sort of congregation (family sized) and the second-to-largest sort of congregation (program sized) are both group-centered types of congregations.

So you might be thinking—are you saying that a bivocational church is going to regress toward being a smaller, family-sized, group-centered congregation?

This much is certainly true: group-centered congregations tend to be better suited for life as bivocational congregations. The dynamic of a community in which groups cohere around ministries, tasks, and critical functions is much more easily aligned with the way a bivocational model of ministry *has* to work—with a genuine sharing of responsibility and authority among all members of the community, lay and ordained.

But here is something else to consider: *All* of the size-defined models of congregations familiar to many who have read books like Rothauge's, Mann's, and other observers of congregational life, are—in some fundamental sense—pastor-centered to begin with. They all presume the existence of the Standard Model of ministry—the pastor-as-full-time-professional, with all the rights and privileges (and costs) that go with that idea. This is not a critique so much as it is stating a fact. Rothauge was writing more than thirty years ago, and summarizing research conducted even earlier. Mann was writing just at the turn of the millennium, now nearly twenty years ago. While their insights are still important and helpful, the dramatic changes in church membership in the first two decades of this century, the rise of the "nones," and the decline in intergenerational transfer of religious tradition and practice (that is, the percentage of children who take up and follow in either the religious practices of their parents or in one of their own choosing)[10] are changing in fundamental ways some of the economic assumptions on which our Standard Model was built.

In a way, *all* Christian faith communities are being pushed toward a more group-centered dynamic, if only because being a part of such a community is no longer something one just does because of social expectation or family tradition. As the church changes in response to broader social shifts, our faith communities will be increasingly characterized by people who are there *by conscious choice*—by an affirmative adherence to the basic claims of the Christian faith and a willingness to live in ways shaped by the expectations of discipleship. What this means is that churches will still be big and small and everything in between, but the people in them will be more likely to be purposeful in their membership and more naturally focused on taking up a part of the work of the community's ministry. And that will mean a general shift toward more group-focused structures and attitudes across all churches—and a changing role, generally, for the ordained minister, one more narrowly focused on the gifts and tasks that truly and rightly distinguish the ordained ministry.

Most of the parishes I visited in the course of my explorations of bivocational ministry neither grew nor shrank once they shifted toward

10. See, for example, Joel Thiessen and Sarah Wilkins-Laflamme, "Becoming a Religious None: Irreligious Socialization and Disaffiliation," *Journal for the Scientific Study of Religion* 56:1 (May 2017), 64–82; DOI: 10.1111/jssr.12319.

this model of ministry. They held their own—which in present circumstances has to be seen as a kind of growth by itself—and grew in ways not measured by numbers of people but by depth of commitment and engagement. Some of them were family sized; some of them were pastoral sized; only one of them was program sized. But *all* of them were, in important ways, group centered. All of them were communities in which initiative and authority were shared among all members. And all of them were places in which pastors had worked consciously to reinscribe their own understanding of the role of ordained leadership within Christian communities.

So What About Us?

You may be reading this book because your own congregation has reached a moment of decision about your future path as a faith community. You may be confronting the impossibility of affording a full-time pastor and wondering whether your community can adapt to the part-time presence of its ordained minister. There are many different forms of part-time pastorates. A bivocational model may prove to be a way for your community to flourish—but as you consider this possibility you should prayerfully consider a few things that seem to distinguish communities that succeed with this approach to ministry. They're the qualities that seem to be more present than absent in congregations I've observed that have made a successful transition to a bivocational model, and have found ways to flourish within it.

Bench depth in the lay leaders of the parish

Bivocational congregations share the work of a community's ministry between lay and ordained members in significant and substantial ways. Often—especially in small, pastor-centered parishes that function like pastoral-sized parishes even if they are actually smaller in number—lay leadership atrophies down to a core group of a dozen or fewer lay leaders who enter into a pattern of swapping necessary jobs and titles among them, unable to recruit other members of the community to take up their part of the work. This is, to say it candidly, a failure of leadership, if only because a key aspect of leadership is to see and affirm the potential contributions of all members of the community and to connect that potential to the work that needs doing.

By contrast, parishes that have relatively strong and capable members willing to make *and keep* commitments to take up part of the work may respond with eagerness to a new structure of ministry in which the ordained member(s) of the congregation has real limits on her (or their) availability and time. In my visits to bivocational communities, I found that the number of people involved, or willing to be involved, in roles of responsibility in the parish tended to be between half and two-thirds of the average Sunday attendance. That's to say, in a parish like mine—which typically sees fifty people on Sunday morning—I could readily count between twenty-five and thirty-three people who could be recruited to take on some ministry of the parish, from the relatively substantial (serving as the treasurer) to the occasional (helping out at the twice-annual work days).

An ethos of problem-solving rather than problem-exploiting

Imagine the following scenario. It's Sunday morning. You discover a leak in the ladies' room sink off the parish hall. Water from the leak is dripping down into a classroom below, used by the nursery school that rents space from the church.

First possibility:

"Didn't someone call the plumber about this?"

"I thought the administrator was going to do it."

"Well, obviously she didn't think it was very important, I guess."

"The nursery school people are going to be bent out of shape about this."

"I keep saying that the plumbing is just so old around here—it all should have been replaced."

"I'm surprised the grounds committee hasn't dealt with this already—they usually just do things without telling anyone else what they're up to."

Second possibility:

"Wow, we need to deal with this. I'll call the plumber and leave a message on his machine—his number is in the contact book."

"You know the nursery school folks better than I do—could you reach out to them?"

"Sure—I'll do it later today, so they're not surprised by this tomorrow."

"I think Joe and I could probably get the water shut off to that sink and at least clean up the area that got damp downstairs."

"That would be great. Thanks so much!"

Most of us who have spent much time at all in churches have experienced moments like both of these examples. Sometimes people show how much they care about something by critiquing the problem; sometimes they show it by imagining solutions. Both approaches can be helpful, but bivocational churches—at least successful and happy ones—tend to have an ethos focused on the second, rather than the first. The questions that spring to mind for just about everyone in the community are more along the lines of "How can I help?" or "What can we do?" rather than "What else can go wrong?" To say it in a single word, bivocational congregations have a strong sense of *agency*—a belief that they can act in response to challenges.

I have a favorite story about this from my own parish. One Sunday morning, with about ten minutes to go before the ten o'clock service and most of us scurrying around with our last-minute preparations, the telephone rang. Anyone who has ever answered a church telephone on Sunday morning knows that the chances are well above 90 percent that the caller on the other end is going to ask, "What time is the service this morning?"

I knew that the outgoing message on the telephone says, among other things, that we have services at eight and ten on Sundays. I also knew that if the phone was ringing and I didn't pick it up, it would be noticed. So I ran over and picked up the phone—to get the predicted result.

The following week at the vestry meeting I shared that story with the lay leadership and concluded by asking, "Should I have answered the phone?"

The responses came from around the table:

"Of course not. That's what the message machine is for."

"But then again . . . what if someone had needed something?"

"What could anyone need at ten minutes to ten on Sunday morning?"

"Still, it seems weird to let the phone just ring with everyone here. . . ."

"But that's a time that Mark shouldn't have to be distracted by the telephone."

No conclusions were reached, no motions were offered or votes taken. But the next Sunday morning, after the eight o'clock crowd had downed their coffee and cleared out, I walked into the office to find Charlie, a member of the vestry, sitting at the desk with his coffee and calmly reading the newspaper. He took in the surprise on my face, turned back to the paper, and simply explained, "I just thought the phone might ring."

I love this little story for a lot of reasons. First, Charlie saw the need and put himself forward to address it. There was no need for a committee, a plan, a task force, or a mission statement. Moreover, because his solution to a clear problem was so eloquently simple, hearing about what he had done caused a small (and, on my part, prayed-for) epiphany to break forth: others began stepping forward in similar ways.

Yet even more important than all of this was the spirit that Charlie's simple act embodied: It is better to act in a way aspiring to solve a problem than in a way tending to complicate it. That sort of spirit turns out to be synergistic for all sorts of good purposes, and it is well worth the effort required to inculcate it—by modeling it, by identifying and affirming it when it happens, and by celebrating its accomplishments.

An appetite for experimentation—and a tolerance for failure

Changing fundamental assumptions about how ministry is structured is not an easy business. It touches the most important aspects of a community's life together—not only requiring shifts in patterns of expectations between the pastor and the members of the community, but rethinking priorities in the budget, relationships with the principal actors outside the community (the city or town, the neighbors, the vendors, the tenants), and the ways in which decisions are approached, made, implemented, and assessed.

All of this requires trying a lot of new things. It requires clarity around what it means when something new "works," and when it doesn't.[11] And it requires a willingness to try things that might fail, to know when they've failed, and learning from, not assigning blame for, those experiences. That seems straightforward—and to anyone who has ever been in a start-up company, it's completely unsurprising.

But the church has very little experience with these values and ideas, at least in the last few centuries. The experience of the Protestant ascendancy in twentieth-century America accustomed us to the idea that what it meant to be a successful church was to be staid, firm, unchanging, and above embarrassment—things we could be (but should not have been) when we were culturally dominant. In those days, our idea of evangelism was, in essence, to put on our best clothes and stand with a smile at the door of the church on Sunday morning. With an inheritance like that, experimentation can feel like selling out important traditions and

_____

11. On creating clear and effective ways of doing this important work, excellent guidance can be found in Sarah Birmingham Drummond, *Holy Clarity: The Practice of Planning and Evaluation* (Herndon, Va.: Alban Institute, 2009).

long-standing ways of making meaning. Even trying new things feels like a silent vote of no confidence in our own inheritance.

To see it that way is to take a very short-sighted view of the history of the church. There are no deep theological commitments involved in who represents the church to the nursery school downstairs or the vendors who pick up the garbage or clean the halls. There's no deep sense of ordained ministry that needs to own those roles. We can imagine different ways of representing the church, different ways of organizing ourselves for the work we must do, even different ways of conducting the liturgy so as to emphasize the equal sharing of responsibility and authority between ordained and lay members. (We gave up the idea of the ordained minister walking up the aisle last in the procession, for example; I walk side-by-side with the Eucharistic minister of the day.)

We can experiment with very basic things—what we call ourselves, and how we describe ourselves to the community around us; how we describe our roles in the church; how we share work among ourselves. At one annual meeting, we imagined what we would call ourselves if for some reason Saint John were suddenly stricken from the roster of saints. It was an interesting exercise, and one that reminded us that the ancient practice of naming churches after saints as a way of appealing to the faithful is perhaps a little bit outmoded in a culture that has little if any grasp of the stories that made those saints so attractive as examples. Not surprisingly, many of the emergent churches have figured this out and acted accordingly; down the street from us is "Elevation Chapel," and near where I work in Amherst, Massachusetts is "Mercy House."

Trying new things means setting down what "success" will mean if an experiment succeeds, how long it might take to evaluate whether success has been achieved, and what resources from the community will be needed to give the experiment the best chances of working. A simple example is the question of starting a new worship service. What resources will it take? Time, yes; perhaps additional support from the parish administrator and the custodians; it may impose slightly increased utility costs. What will "success" look like? Will it be a minimum attendance, or growth in the overall average Sunday attendance? Will it be some additional, less quantifiable quality? At what point after the experiment begins will it be appropriate to take stock about what impact it has had on the community, both in terms of benefits and costs? A month? A season? A year?

A clear sense of the community's spiritual charism

If each congregation has a distinct personality, then each congregation receives from God a unique set of spiritual gifts. Said differently, each faith community is blessed with its own distinct charism—a quality, or depth of skill, at certain aspects of ministry.

Most of us have an idea of what a church does that comes from an experience of relatively large churches. A church offers a beautiful service of worship with a range of music. It offers Christian formation for people at all life stages. It offers pastoral care to those who are ill or in life transitions. It provides outreach to those in need. It works to bring people who are outside the church or unaffiliated with any faith community into the embrace of the community. It witnesses to the claims of the gospel in the world.

Smaller churches often feel weighed down by a sense that they lack the resources to do all these things. Often, a result—sometimes amplified, consciously or otherwise, by the attitudes of the larger polity or denominational structure—is that they question the legitimacy of their ministry. My experiences with congregations succeeding in a bivocational structure of ministry nearly always included a story about focusing on the things the community did well, and being less concerned about being a full-service spiritual supermarket. Some parishes had a beautiful liturgical tradition, and became "destination churches" for the quality of that observance. Some had strong preaching traditions. Some have creative expressions of liturgy—a praise service, a Celtic worship service, a contemplative service. Others were more centered in outreach to those in need, and drew their identity, sense of purpose, and energy from that focus. Others had strong gifts for inclusion and welcome, becoming communities where acceptance becomes the rule by which other expressions of ministry are shaped.

The point is that when the structure of ministry in these communities shifted, either of necessity or choice, to a bivocational model, the work began with asking—and praying on—a fundamental question: What have we been gifted to do? What are we good at? A different way to ask this is—what do we find real joy in doing together? Whatever that strength is, in it lives a clue from the Giver of all gifts as to the purpose to which God is calling that community.

Financial stability

The good news is that a shift from the Standard Model to a bivocational model can have immediate, and generally positive, impact on the finances of a faith community. Think of it this way: In 2015, the Episcopal Church reported that the median total compensation for a full-time priest in the smallest-sized (family sized) parish was $59,847.[12] Allowing for modest inflation since then, let's say that number is now $60,000. On top of that, imagine that the full-time cleric depends on the church for access to health insurance. Conservatively, the costs of that to the parish will be about 30 percent of the total salary, or an additional $18,000. And then—at least in the Episcopal Church—the parish will be required to contribute 18 percent of the cleric's total compensation toward a pension plan; there's another $10,800. Our "Standard Model" cleric now costs nearly $89,000—and that's the lowest part of the range.

---

12. Church Pension Group, "The 2015 Church Compensation Report," 3; July 2016. https://www.cpg.org/linkservid/52804A0F-D7BE-3E5F-DFC951500B70F3C2/showMeta/0/.

There is nothing wrong—let's be clear—about a ministry that involves full-time professionals. But it is not clear that this should be the norm in all cases, much less the standard of what constitutes a church. So let's construct a different example. If that same church were to decide on a bivocational model for ministry, they might hire an ordained person on a part-time basis. Let's assume that this person has another job that provides them with access to health care benefits. That means they'll likely have to work at least 70 percent of their time for that employer. They'll have only 30 percent of their time to give to their work in ministry, and that 30 percent will be a pretty strong upward limit on the time they have available.

But it also means that the compensation for this person will now be more like $18,000. There won't need to be a 30 percent addition for health insurance, although some additional payment to help pay for health care may be opted for. The pension contribution will still need to be provided for—here, $3,240. The total cost for ordained leadership in the community would thus be $21,240—or just about a quarter of what it was in the Standard Model.

This scale of change can help a parish stabilize its finances, but it *cannot* be the solution to a problem of chronic underfunding. If the parish is consistently drawing down capital from its endowment to balance the books at the end of the year—essentially, regarding those funds as a savings account, rather than a source of additional income—then a deeper problem is present, one unlikely to be addressed with a change in ministry models. If the income generated from active members of the parish—those giving through annual or consistent gifts—is not sufficient to cover the operational costs of the congregation, that can be a warning sign as well.

In the case of my own parish, the change in ministry models meant that the income from pledges provided more than we needed to pay for all members of the staff. (It also meant that the rector was no longer the highest-compensated member of the staff.) The building was made to pay for the costs of running the building (through rental income). The income from endowment was turned to other purposes in ministry, as well as catching up on deferred capital improvements to our century-old building. Our financial health has improved—and our numbers have grown, modestly, in the period since we implemented our model.

A set of needs outside the doors that the community strives to serve

Archbishop William Temple famously quipped, "The church is the only society that exists for the benefit of those who are not its members." The truth of this statement is so deep that it may also be stated in the inverse: A society that does not exist for the benefit of those who are not its members may be many things, but it cannot be a church. To be a church means to have ways of identifying and serving the needs of those *outside* the doors. There is no limit to the ways in which this can be done. It can be through contributions of funds, of food to the local pantry, or of time to voluntary societies serving the needs of others. It can be through mission trips or through pastoral outreach to the homebound. It can be through the creation of sanctuary space or other forms of support for refugees. But there must be some form of outreach. A gathering of disciples is distinguished by its work to reach beyond its own membership to address the needs of the world beyond its own.

A shift to a bivocational model of ministry typically brings with it a reorganization of the financial commitments and priorities of a faith community. That brings as well a moment of opportunity for the community to identify, and focus renewed resources toward, an outreach beyond its own walls. It may well be that the need is just across the street, or down the block. Searching out and addressing such needs can give a smaller faith community a sense of real and substantial accomplishment, which in turn can help strengthen confidence and a sense of holy purpose. Or there may be a historic connection between the parish and a mission need more globally defined, one that might be bolstered with new resources, energy, and vision.

An awareness of its own understanding of leadership

At the close of the previous chapter we looked at how questions of identity intersect with the exercise of authority by an individual leader. The forces shaping our identity are both individual and social; some aspects of our identity are determined by our genetic inheritance, some we choose for ourselves, and some are imposed on us by cultural narratives and socially constructed expectations.

Communities, as well as individuals, have identities. A congregation may think of (and speak of) itself as a working-class congregation; a black church; an Anglo-Catholic parish; an urban, suburban, or rural congregation; a welcoming community; or any one of a number of other familiar phrases we use to describe ourselves, each one of which is layered with meaning.

Because leadership is inescapably a social phenomenon, how a given congregation responds to the particular demands of a bivocational pastorate—and to the skills and gifts of a particular bivocational pastor—will be shaped by aspects of that community's identity. The history of leadership style matters. A congregation may have a long tradition of strong, top-down leadership; that will form part of its identity, set the terms of what it expects leaders to do, and create both opportunities and challenges for whomever steps in to offer a bivocational model of pastoral ministry. So, too, the history of how the community came to be matters; a congregation may be in an urban, historically working-class community, in which a certain group (or groups) has long had a strong presence in the congregation, groups that have their own culturally shaped understanding of how leadership looks and sounds.

It's important to make clear that this is not an observation about "good" and "bad" forms of leadership. There are plenty of examples of both across all leadership styles, and all varieties of communities. All leadership in the church is subject the understanding that it serves a holy purpose: helping individual believers find and express in the fullest possible way their unique baptismal gifts, and building up from these individuals a gathered community of believers and fellow-ministers who work to proclaim, and live by, the call of the gospel. But this way of describing the purpose of leadership leaves open a wide latitude of possibility for the Holy Spirit in bringing together individual pastors, with their particular gifts, needs, identities, and ways of expressing leadership, with individual communities, which equally have their own blessed particularities.

Ultimately, leadership is both empowered and bound by the realities of the social context in which it is exercised. Congregations that are on the path of considering shifting toward a bivocational model of ministry do well to begin with thoughtful reflection on how leadership has been exercised throughout the history of the community, both by ordained and lay leaders. This really is an exercise of raising what are nearly always subconscious and unspoken realities to a conscious and explicit level: How does the community itself understand and respond to different styles of ministry? What are the ways in which the community perceives the intersections of personal identity with expected (and accepted) expressions of leadership style? A congregation that hopes to move in the direction of a bivocational expression of ministry, but has a longstanding history of being strongly pastor-centered in both its own identity and its decision-making patterns, may well have difficulty adjusting to the sharing of both responsibility and identity in ministry characteristic of bivocational parish life.

One last word of caution: These qualities are indicators of the sort of congregations that can successfully adapt to, and thrive as, bivocational communities. They're not guarantees of an ability to do so. Transitions are always difficult, and can be fraught with risk, the potential for loss, and the prospect of disappointment.

But there are significant advantages to growing into a bivocational community. The growth of all members in the ministry of the community moves significantly from an interesting idea to a vivid reality. The gifts of and need for the ordained ministry become clearer as its purpose is focused and clarified. The resources of the community can be reimagined and reorganized. And the whole of the community takes a higher sense of ownership in the life and work of the church—which is, as it turns out, a key component of a church that is poised for growth.

Chapter 3
The Bivocational Polity

The e-mail came in the midst of a busy Monday at work. It popped up in my inbox as I was taking notes at a meeting:

> **Subject: Clericus on Wednesday—advance reading**
> Dear Colleagues,
> I have heard from some of you regarding your in/ability to be with us on Wednesday. If you haven't yet rsvp'd (whether or not you can make it), please do so today, so our host church has some time to prepare.
> In preparation for our time together, Karen has prepared a paper for us to read in advance of our time together. Nick will also present before we begin our conversation.
> I have attached the document from Karen. Please do not share it without permission.
> Many thanks, and I look forward to seeing you tomorrow at Clergy Day.
> Peace,
>
> Jeff+

Some context is perhaps in order to understand what this message was asking me to do. Like most ordained pastors, I work within the context of a denomination. That denomination is shaped around a Christian tradition—in my case, the American expression of the Anglican tradition, itself one of the five broad expressions of the Reformation. But it is also an organizational structure in which an understanding of how authority should work in the church is reflected.

In the case of my own tradition, as a pastor in a parish, I ultimately answer to the authority of my bishop. But between my work in the parish and the bishop's position as the head of the diocese is another, mid-level structure—the deanery. (This is not necessarily true of all Episcopal dioceses.) In my case, the deanery is defined in terms of watersheds: our deaneries are named after rivers. The deanery has a dean, who is the rector of one of the churches in the group. The dean has certain responsibilities delegated by the bishop, one of which is to encourage a practice of collegiality among the ordained ministers of the faith communities within the deanery. And the usual form this takes is a once-a-month meeting over lunch, which rotates between the various churches.

It's a lovely idea. More than that, it's an important way to facilitate a degree of mutual support and accountability among people devoted to the work of the church and the health of their respective communities. But it's completely unworkable if you're a bivocational minister who, like me, works some distance away from their parish—in my case, sixty-eight miles. I was being asked to come to the monthly lunch the day *after* an annual day-long gathering of all clergy in the diocese. I hadn't missed that—but it cost me a vacation day from my other job to be sure I could be there. For the lunch, though, I had to send my regrets. I've had to miss nearly every one of those lunches. I tried at one point to suggest that perhaps our clericus meetings might take place occasionally in the evening. My colleagues took that idea on board, but in the end, the dean explained, "There just wasn't a lot of interest in that idea. You know, family time is important to folks." Ah, well.

❖

Much of the life of the church—not just Sunday morning, and not just the management and organization of a single congregation—is built around the assumption that the ordained members of the faith community will not just be members of a profession, but professionals—people whose work life and economic life are characterized by being full-time employees of the church. A regular meeting of colleagues in ministry taking place at a weekday lunch assumes at least two things: First, that everyone works near their church because they *only* work for the church; and second, that everyone can take the time to gather for the purpose, because their working time is given *only* to the church.

Imagine organizing a regular monthly meeting between the lay members of the governing boards of churches within a given town, who are no less ministers of the church. Almost certainly you would not organize that meeting on a weekday—at least not if it happened in the middle of the day. That's because you would begin with the understanding that, although they are ministers, they also have obligations during the workday. Yet for an increasing number of the ordained members of our communities, the same thing turns out to be true.

A lot of good has come from the professionalization of ordained ministers. There are similar expectations across traditions and denominations for the educational preparation ministers will have before they are ordained. (No longer is it the case that the bishops have to publish sermons for clergy to read on Sunday morning—as Bishops Cranmer and Jewel did in the first years after the English church split from Rome, because most priests were simply unable to write their own.) There are expectations around work experience that those moving toward ordination should gain—experiences working in the setting of a faith community or as a chaplain in a pastoral setting. And there are systems to attend to the problems that come about when ordained people behave in ways inconsistent with the particular responsibilities of their work in the church—disciplinary canons, for example.

Ministry as a profession dates back to the early modern period, when it was viewed as one of the three "learned professions" alongside medicine and the law. These were distinct roles offering services necessary to society, and for which a relatively significant degree of education was required. But over the course of the industrial age, which saw a tremendous growth in specializations requiring training and emerging as distinct occupations, the idea of ordained ministry somehow became identified with the profession itself, and, more specifically, with an economic expression of that profession—a full-time occupation.

Even so, the professionalized notion of the ordained ministry was not always the case in the United States. Early on in the history of the nation, when the culture was considerably more theocentric, ordained ministers were viewed as people who held a public office; they were chosen and paid by the people in a given town. By the mid-1800s the role of the church in society had significantly changed, and its sphere was understood to be limited to the role of private conscience, not public administration. As Donald Scott has written, "By the 1850s the clergy was no longer framed by its role and position in the local community but was shaped by a new kind of translocal structure [i.e., a denominational polity] and professional consciousness."[13]

It could be said that this increasing "professional consciousness" was a way in which the church asserted the case that its ordained leaders should be accorded the respect and social stature given to other professions. And it should be no surprise that the economic institutions that express in substantive ways the authority structures of denominational polities were strongly influenced in their development by the corporate structures that emerged as industrial organization matured. These structures are well-suited for rationalizing costs, assuring consistency in the performance of socially significant functions, and developing equitable treatment for

---

13. Donald M. Scott, *From Office to Profession*, 154.

similarly trained and similarly employed professionals across a nation growing in both population and geography. But in important ways, they simultaneously constrain our ways of thinking about and living out the work of the ordained members of our faith communities—and restrict our imagination for adapting to a changing future.

The emergence of bivocational communities will make new demands on denominational structures created for the most part in the late nineteenth and early twentieth centuries. They will pose new questions—about how the life of the church is ordered; about the qualifications and qualities to be sought in candidates for ordained ministry; about how authority can be structured in ways consistent with both the purposes of God and new realities for the church; even about how the relationship of authority and hierarchy might be reimagined for a moment in which the most successful and innovative organizations are nimble, flat, and far more focused on functions and outcomes than on titles and process. We can anticipate at least three ways in which bivocational communities push against the long-standing routines and preferences of our denominational polities:

The sharing of authority between ordained and lay members of the church

In virtually all churches, and certainly in Protestant churches, the understanding of authority begins with the gifts conferred on all people in baptism. The gathered community of the baptized is called to undertake its ministry by aligning itself with God's purposes in whatever circumstances they find themselves. That ministry is carried out by the expression of the authority all members have received in baptism, and guided by the understanding of God's purposes as the church has received it through its traditions, reflections on scripture, and engagement with the world.

Ordination in the church has long been understood to confer on those ordained certain kinds of authority, to be exercised on behalf and within the context of the community of faith. Ordination is not meant to be a means of conferring a "Good Housekeeping Seal of Approval" on the spiritual maturity of an individual—although it is too often mistaken, and sought, as such. It is predicated on the context of Christian community, a community within which the expression of this particular authority can meaningfully be expressed. Across various traditions this authority can be expressed in a variety of specific ways. It can mean the authority to shape and direct the worship experience of the community; to pronounce absolution of those who have confessed sins; to preside at sacramental functions (specifically to bless the elements in the Eucharist, to pronounce the nuptial blessing at weddings, to offer prayers of healing, and to bless the people); to preach, or more generally to serve as the principal teacher of the community; and to read from the gospels under certain circumstances of worship.

Beyond these, however, there are a variety of expressions or signs of authority that have rather less substance and are the accumulated perquisites of custom. Think of clerical collars, or the use of the honorific "The Reverend" and its various combinations, or the practice of signing one's name with a cross. These are forms of professional distinction, like calling your physician "Doctor" or addressing the judge as "Your Honor." They are meant to signify authority. But they also serve to create distance between the members of the faith community and one particular kind of member (the ordained). If we consider them thoughtfully, it is not always clear how it is possible to reconcile these practices with the task of carrying out a ministry in the name of a gospel that teaches the radical equality of all people, and is set in the terms of a story about a God who cares so much for people that the personhood of God takes on flesh and lives among us in order to collapse all that separates us.

Bivocational communities are communities that are intentional and thoughtful about the purpose, and sharing, of authority. They understand that there is a need and a role for ordained ministry in any Christian community, but they are willing—both lay people *and ordained people*—to examine with care the purpose and effectiveness of the kinds of authority traditionally handed over to the pastor in congregational life. And they are willing to ask how much of that comes not from the wisdom of the Spirit but from the accretion of custom into something posing as doctrine, or from the unspoken desire to concentrate in one person the broader responsibility for the community's ministry that all should share.

The challenge for denominational structures—which, after all, are first and foremost systems for shaping the rules by which authority is expressed in the life of the church—will be to create space for, and have patience with, this kind of questioning and exploration. Polities can encourage the emergence of strong bivocational communities in a number of ways—by providing resources (funding, expertise, pastoral support), but even more significantly by resisting the reflex to solve problems or create solutions from the top. Viable, Spirit-filled, innovative answers to the "question of the future of the church"—of which bivocational communities are only one—are far more likely to grow from the bottom up, and not be dispensed from the top down. It is one thing to say this; it is another, harder thing to shape practice and process around it.

The identification and formation of those chosen for ordained ministry and the nature of the community they share

Central among the purposes for which denominational structures are created are the functions of identifying, forming, and certifying the readiness of those who are called to an ordained vocation in the church. The balance of responsibility between the local congregation and the denominational polity varies from tradition to tradition when it comes to identifying and raising up individuals for ordained vocations; but for the most part it is for the polity to establish screening processes, articulate qualifications, and prescribe requirements for entrance into the ordained ministry.

Not surprisingly, the dominant model of how that ministry is expressed has historically wielded considerable influence in shaping the qualifications regarded as essential, and the qualities regarded as desirable, in candidates for the ordained ministry. To say it in sharper language, if the way in which we construct the ordained ministry is exclusively as professional occupation, then it will tend to be the case that we look for candidates who see the highest purpose of the church as the building up of the institution of the church—and not necessarily the transformation of the lives of its members.

Like most of the bivocational pastors I met, my view of the church is more instrumental than institutional. What I mean by that—and what I see lived out in the lives of bivocational communities in real and transformational ways—is that the church is a means, not an end; it is the means by which lives are transformed by the message of the Gospel and the experience of being part of a gospel-centric community. It is, in short, a contingent structure, not a permanent one. If it does not accomplish the purposes for which God has brought it into being, God will work in some other way to accomplish God's purposes. On this view, more fully developed in the next chapter, the church is not the purpose of our life of faith; our purpose is to remake the world in terms of God's plans, not to build an alternative reality called "the church" at a safe remove from the world.

The sort of people I've observed who live out a bivocational ordained ministry effectively and magnetically are people who do not see the church as a refuge, but as a refueling station—a place for reflection, renewal, and rededication, but not for residence. They are comfortable with the public identity of being a Christian in the secular world, without a need for the trappings of ordained life to receive deference or achieve distinction. To use an old word, their ministry is, at its core, apologetic—an idea that presupposes living in the borderlands between the church and the world as yet beyond its reach. By walking through the world in secular roles as "out Christians," they provide powerful leadership by example, encouraging all ministers in their community—ordained or lay—to do the same.

To find more such people we'd look for potential candidates for ministry who see the professional skills and experiences they bring as enriching their understanding of, and work in, an ordained role. We'd look for people who have career paths in professions that they value, perform well in, and wish to pursue alongside their work as an ordained member of their communities. We'd see that the fact they wish to be bivocational is not a sign of a less-than-serious commitment to the demands and expectations of ordained ministry, or to the life of the church. We'd understand that it might rather be that they bring with them a different understanding of how the ministry of the church can adapt to the demands of new circumstances, and a sense of how their own gifts for ministry might offer something creative and constructive in advancing that ministry.

In years past, commissions on ministry, annual conferences, presbyteries, candidacy committees, and similar entities sought those who brought, together with the needed skills and spiritual maturity for ordination, a desire to become wholly a part of the life of the church. It's this last bit that came to distinguish the Standard Model: a person who, somewhat prosaically, not only had the capabilities required for ordained ministry but who fit the working culture of the church as well. But the world has changed. Consider these lines from a guidance document set before people inquiring into ministry in the Presbyterian Church:

> . . . these questions about self-understanding in the context of ministry need to be paired with frank and honest conversations about the current realities of pastoral ministry within the Presbyterian Church. For example, a sizable majority of most Presbyterians—and so, not surprisingly, most inquirers—belong to congregations with more than 250 members. However, a majority of our churches have fewer than 100 members, and many are in rural areas or inner-city neighborhoods.

Such congregations often do not have budgets that can support salary and compensation packages in keeping with presbytery-set minimums for full-time pastoral positions. Additionally, one current trend within the church is the formation of smaller faith communities that may be intentionally smaller than 100 members as a means for maintaining mutual accountability in their discipleship. Is the inquirer willing and able to consider ministry with churches quite different from the congregations where they may belong? Is the inquirer willing and able to accept a call that may require both relocation to another area *and pairing pastoral ministry with other forms of work to make the arrangement economically viable?*[14]

This is a statement of admirable candor from the very highest level of a denominational polity, acknowledging—if not quite welcoming—the reality of bivocational communities as a path toward the church's future. It invites us to think about the qualities and skills we might look for in candidates for ministry who would answer to those challenges affirmatively and willingly.

Unlike candidates of the past, they will neither be interested in, nor necessarily suited for, the church as a working culture. They will have demonstrated a clear capacity for leadership and the creativity, focus, and charisma that align with entrepreneurial skill. They will be passionate about connecting the message and life of the church to the world's needs, and perhaps would have demonstrated skills for doing so in their ministry before ordination. They will show a capability to balance stewardship of the church's traditions with a willingness to reimagine received structures and question assumptions about their purposes and processes. Their experiences and personal inclinations will give evidence that the focus of their approach to the work of ministry would be more on outcomes than on process, more on creating solutions than maintaining structures. They

---

14. "Deciding about 'suitability for ordered ministry,'" *Advisory Handbook on Preparation for Ministry PC (USA)*, June 2015, 42; emphasis added.

will, in short, be guided in their understanding of the call of the church to ministry in the years ahead by the warning of Jesus at the end of the parable of the wicked tenants: "Therefore I tell you, the kingdom of God will be taken away from you, and given to a people that produces the fruits of the kingdom" (Matthew 21:43).

There is one additional consideration that poses a considerable challenge to the institutional structures we have received. It is the difficulty of seeing ordained ministry as *one* thing, with *one* kind of function or purpose in God's gathered community, even though it is expressed in economically different ways. Said differently, it's the difficulty of all ordained members of the church to understand that they share a common calling regardless of the nature of their appointment.

This tension can find expression in difficult, sometimes hurtful ways. The emergence of new models of ministry that are at a variance with the received expectation of a full-time professional occupation can seem to question the legitimacy of older models, or find us falling into that one singular proof of the doctrine of original sin—our insistence on rank-ordering each other. The difficulty became very real for the members of Saint Luke's, Hastings, who were raised up for ordination, mentioned at the outset of the previous chapter. They found that at least some of their new colleagues in ministry among the diocesan clergy were not at all prepared to receive them as equals, and even sought to ensure that they would not be permitted to function as ordained people outside their own parish. As it turned out, their bishop made it clear to all clergy that there were no second-class priests in the diocese.

There is an unlikely, perhaps surprising, but potentially instructive example for denominational polities to look to in creating a feeling of common purpose and vocation across the ranks of full-time and bivocational clergy. That example is—believe it or not—the military. For decades, the armed forces have created a leadership cadre of officers comprising both full-time, active-duty members of the armed services, and officers in various forms of the armed forces reserve. As of 2015, out of a total of nearly 390,000 officers in the American military, roughly 59.25 percent are full-time, active-duty military members, while 40.75 percent are in some form of the ready reserve—and working in other jobs.

That said, when it comes to the purpose of their profession—being deployed to the front lines—there is no distinction in the authority or the responsibility of these officers in the performance of their duties. They understand themselves to be part of one profession, sharing one purpose, and formed by one ethos.

Achieving a similar sort of outcome for ordained pastors in an increasing variety of professional roles and settings is a leadership task for denominational polities. Permitting a system of rank or class to emerge between full-time and part-time pastors, bivocational or otherwise, is tantamount to saying that the faithful in smaller or group-centered congregations served by non-full-time pastors are somehow second-class as well. Leaders of denominations have the responsibility to reimagine ways of working in the church in order create a deeper sense of common purpose and a greater degree of genuine equity between all ordained ministers serving faith communities.

Practical steps toward this end might encompass everything from choices about who gets seen as a candidate for governance roles in the polity to the time meetings are scheduled and the ways participation is engaged. (In my work outside the church, nearly all of my meetings are held by videoconference—enabling my colleagues to organize a common work involving people across the country.) If we were to project imaginatively the upside-down ideas of the gospel onto church life—the kingdom Jesus describes where the first come last, life comes out of death, the marginal are central in concern, and the servant is the leader—we might construct a new vision of Christian community in which bivocational communities were the standard and norm, and communities that needed full-time professionals to lead them would be the cause of concern and worry.

The understanding of, and teaching about, ordained ministry in the life of the church

The emergence of bivocational communities reflects a response to the dramatically changed circumstances of the church in society, circumstances that many Standard Model churches have not yet addressed. These twentieth-century institutional structures, carrying out nineteenth-century ideas of ministry, are often neither capable nor willing to rethink and reframe the role of ordained clergy to adapt to the needs of the twenty-first century church.

In the following chapter we'll look more deeply at a theological approach to an understanding of the purposes of ordained ministry within the Christian community. Here, our focus is more on the practical consideration of adapting the structures of the church to a world unimaginable even to those who built the castles of America's Protestant ascendancy a century ago.

The challenges we face are not just cultural; they're not just technological; they're not just intellectual; they're not just economic. They are all of these together, and more besides. At the deepest level they reflect a dislocation in our sense of the spiritual in our lives—or of God's place in our world. They undermine our capacity for community building, as we retreat behind the glow of our individual screens. They confuse connectivity for authentic connection. And they are shifting our ways of organizing to be focused on purposes or causes, not on institutions. Set in these terms, it's plain that the structures of church we have inherited are poorly suited for this set of challenges. To a world accomplishing more and more by commons-based "peer production," we offer hierarchical structures that insist on respect.[15] To a world increasingly suspicious of the claims of

---

15. "Commons-based peer production" is a phrase drawn from Yochai Benkler's insightful *The Wealth of Networks: How Social Production Transforms Markets and Freedom* (New Haven, CT: Yale University Press, 2006).

any institution to legitimacy, we offer a story about a five-hundred-year-old history of institution building.

When the ministry was one of the very few "learned professions," it commanded a kind of deferential respect from people both within and outside the church. That deference arose from the notion that the ordained minister had obtained a body of knowledge that conferred a kind of power over one's spiritual well-being, in the same way the doctor's knowledge conferred power over our physical well-being, or the lawyer's knowledge conferred power over our political well-being. But this has now fundamentally changed. Doctors still know more about our bodies than we do, and lawyers still know more about the law than we do—and we have a great deal at stake in both our physical and political well-being. But having their spiritual lives in order no longer seems quite as urgent to most people—even to people in the church. For many it is little more than a kind of moral therapy, not a profoundly consequential struggle between good and evil fought on the battleground of our souls. What's more, it's no longer self-evident that the minister possesses any particular authority, at least not authority dispensed by a secular institutional structure over eternal consequences.

The question we must grapple with, then is a profound one: What is the nature of the authority of the ordained ministry in a moment that nearly all of the *church's* claims to authority—claims we simply took for granted not so long ago—have either been revealed as unfounded or subjected to suspicion? Said in different words, if all our claims to authority were shown to be empty, what would the role of the ordained minister be in the context of Christian community?

Dietrich Bonhoeffer, the twentieth-century German theologian and martyr to Nazism, is perhaps the best guide we might find to the work and functioning of Christian community under these circumstances. For Bonhoeffer, the failure of the institutional church and its unsuitability to achieve God's purposes on earth had been revealed in the willingness of the church in Germany to align itself with Nazism in a desperate bid to retain its social prominence and privileges. In his last writings, gathered by his editor and friend Eberhard Bethge as *Letters and Papers from Prison*, Bonhoeffer mused on how Christian community would continue to move forward in history stripped of the power—and the pretentions—of its institutional forms and structures:

> . . . if we had finally to put down the western pattern of Christianity as a mere preliminary stage to doing without religion altogether, what situation would result for us, for the church? How can Christ become the Lord even of those with no religion? If religion is no more than the garment of Christianity—and even that garment has had very different aspects at different periods—then what is a religionless Christianity? . . . For the religionless working man, or indeed, man generally, nothing that makes any real difference is gained by that. The questions needing answers would surely be: What is the significance of a Church (church parish, preaching, Christian life) in a religionless world? How do we speak of God without religion. . . ? How do we speak (but perhaps we are no longer capable of speaking of such things as we used to) in secular fashion of God? In what way are we in a religionless and secular sense Christians, in what way are we the *Ekklesia*, "those who are called forth," not conceiving of ourselves religiously as specially favored but as wholly belonging to the world? Then Christ is no longer an object of religion, but something quite different, indeed and in truth the Lord of the world.[16]

For those of us who love the church and have been shaped for good by its work, these can be unsettling, even sorrowing, words. But it's hard not to glimpse our present moment in these words written more than seventy years ago. What Bonhoeffer makes clear is that, while the institutional structures of religion may rise and fall, the *church*—as the *Ekklesia*, the gathered community of those called after the name of Christ, those who

---

16. Dietrich Bonhoeffer, letter to Eberhard Bethge, April 30, 1944; in Bethge, ed., *Letters and Papers from Prison,* trans. Reginald H. Fuller (New York: Macmillan, 1953), 122–3.

willingly take up the work and identity of disciples, those who together make up the community called forth on God's behalf into the midst of a world incapable of belief—will endure. It will endure because, rather than offer Christ as an object for veneration, it follows after him and reveals him to others as the source of truth.

Bivocational communities are emerging in our context as lived experiences of the church alive and at work without the trappings of authority and the pretensions of power that we once thought were our inheritance. At the center of their identity as communities is a willingness to place everything under interrogation, and to ask how it serves the message of Christ in the world of which Christ is the sovereign. And they do so with a new expectation that the structures of authority we create, and the patterns of community we weave together, must themselves be consistent with the basic claims of the message of radical equality, human dignity, and the profound virtue of humility at the foundation of Christian community.

Through their willingness to reassess and reconfigure the sharing of authority and responsibility in the work of Christian community, bivocational congregations are returning to much earlier patterns in the building up of Christian life and witness in a world that is not dominated by Christian culture nor sympathetic to its claims, its ideas, or its hopes. They are, perhaps not surprisingly, much like the very first communities of Christians. They have a much clearer, if narrower, understanding of the authority set apart for the particular ministry of ordained people, and a much broader understanding of the identity and responsibility all members of the community of disciples must share. The similarity is not surprising because—despite the vast capabilities of our technology, the immense reach of our communications, or the great growth in the general welfare of the planet's population over the past two millennia—the world upon which we have entered is far more like the world of Christianity's first few centuries than any time since. We are returning to patterns of pre-institutional discipling communities because those patterns turn out to work well in a world indifferent or hostile to our faith.

Scholars of leadership distinguish between formal and informal sources of authority: the authority of titles, rank, and custom on the one side, and the authority of charisma, authenticity, and influence on the other. In the realm of international relations, the distinction is sometimes thought of it terms of "hard power" (force) and "soft power" (influence). In the Standard Model of ministry, much of the authority of ordained ministers is derived from formal sources of authority (they were quite literally "ordered" into distinctive ranks of authority). But in emerging bivocational communities, the authority of ordained ministers derives much more from informal sources: from the transparency of their spiritual lives, through and in which all members of the community can find a salutary example of a life transformed by God's grace; from the discipline of their prayer lives, and their openness with the struggles they may have with their own doubts and despairs; from the authenticity of their communication, and the alignment of the pattern of their lives with the gospel they proclaim. Authority in these communities is much more organic and context-specific. In bivocational communities, all have something to learn and all have something to teach. It's the unique task of the ordained minister, not to claim all of the authority for teaching and leadership, but to create a community in which this more mutual sharing of gifts can flourish and grow.

In my first years of ordained ministry, my work was divided between running a research center and working as a minister in a non-denominational church, both situated in a university. When the annual convention of my diocese came around each November, I'd try—often not very hard— to arrange my schedule so that I could knock off work a little early on Friday to go into Boston where the gatherings were typically held.

One year I made excuse after excuse to delay my departure, until finally I arrived at the convention so late that I had to stand against the wall at the very back of the room. Next to me, as it turned out, was a person I had come greatly to admire for her ministry among the homeless in Boston—Debbie Little Wyman, a woman who started a non-profit called Ecclesia Ministries and who had created a weekly Sunday service outdoors on Boston Common for the city's homeless population. Debbie didn't work in a church; she was bivocational, in the sense that she was a social entrepreneur who started a non-profit to do something she thought disciples were called to do.

I don't remember what was on the agenda at the moment I came in. What I do remember, however, is that it was a matter of heated debate—perhaps a resolution about world peace, or environmental stewardship, or the treatment of immigrants, or the formula for calculating parish payments to the diocese. All worthy causes, to be sure, but the crowded room had fallen into bitter division as the contending perspectives lined up at two microphones to lob verbal grenades at each other.

We stood there next to each other, leaning against the back wall, for half an hour or so. Finally, during a break between speeches, Debbie leaned over to me and quietly asked a simple question: "What does any of this have to do with the man on the donkey?"

As I said, I've long since completely forgotten what the argument was about. But I have never forgotten that question, and I never will. "What does any of this have to do with the man on the donkey?" It was a question asked by a woman with profound informal authority as a disciple and, incidentally, as an ordained minister, despite the fact that she had no title, no office, no building, no vestments, practically no budget, and no formal status as a minister in a congregation. But the power of her example—of willingly going without all of the protections and pretenses of those formal sources of authority to live fully into a ministry completely aligned with the call to feed the hungry, clothe the naked, care for the sick, and visit the imprisoned—gave her unchallengeable authority to ask such a question about the operations of the formal structures of the church.

"What does any of this have to do with the man on the donkey?" It is a strong, clarifying, powerful question. It is a question we must ask ourselves as disciples, as communities of the faithful, and as institutional religious structures. It is a question the leaders of our denominational polities must ask in a moment of change and challenge, even if the answers mean surrendering prestige, precedence, and power for the sake of clearing a path for God's message to move into the world. If we ask it faithfully, it will become easier—not easy, but easier—to give up things that seem precious but are weighing us down, things that have become old in order to grasp that which is new.

Chapter 4
The Church: A Bivocational Theology of Ministry

Chapter XLII.—The order of ministers in the Church.

The apostles have preached the Gospel to us from the Lord Jesus Christ; Jesus Christ [has done so] from God. Christ therefore was sent forth by God, and the apostles by Christ. Both these appointments, then, were made in an orderly way, according to the will of God. Having therefore received their orders, and being fully assured by the resurrection of our Lord Jesus Christ, and established in the word of God, with full assurance of the Holy Ghost, they went forth proclaiming that the kingdom of God was at hand. And thus preaching through countries and cities, they appointed the first-fruits [of their labors], having first proved them by the Spirit, to be bishops and deacons of those who should afterwards believe. Nor was this any new thing, since indeed many ages before it was written concerning bishops and deacons. For thus saith the Scripture in a certain place, "I will appoint their bishops in righteousness, and their deacons in faith."

—Clement, First Epistle to the Corinthians

From the earliest generations of Christian community, the way in which authority should be structured within the community (also known as the church) has been a matter of reflection, discussion, and disagreement. The apostles, those followers of Jesus who became the founders of the first Christian communities, were generally seen as the source of authority in shaping the status, direction, and future of the church. As the theologian Harvey Cox has observed, " . . . it did not take long for succeeding generations . . . in the Christian movement to devise the idea of an inherited 'apostolic authority,' even though the apostles themselves had never claimed to hand on any such authority." Cox offers a view both straightforward and sad as to why this authority was both devised and claimed by those who came after: "The reason has to do with the all too human obsession with acquiring and holding on to power."[17]

Harsh though that assessment may be, it is difficult to disagree with. Indeed, what Cox is pointing out is only one expression among many of another theological claim that lies at the foundation of our faith—the notion of our fallenness. There are few more predictable ways in which our unruly wills go off the rails than in seeking, securing, and protecting power, whatever form it might take. As Immanuel Kant famously wrote, "Out of the crooked timber of humanity, no straight thing was ever made"—not a political order, not an economic order, and not, as it turns out, a church.

There are really two questions, separate but intertwined, that we must address if we take up the question of how the church itself, and more specifically how our theological reasoning about the meaning and purpose of ministry in the church, contends with the idea of bivocational ministry. Universally and across traditions we speak of a "vocation" to ministry, a sense of being called into the specific roles and responsibilities reserved to those who are set "in an orderly way"—to quote Clement, an early bishop of Rome to whom authorship of the Epistle to the Corinthians

---

17. Harvey Cox, *The Future of Faith* (New York: HarperOne, 2009), 88.

was ascribed—in the life of the church. But can that vocation coexist with another? Can it be lived out alongside the claims and responsibilities of other work in a different sphere? And even more deeply, what is the purpose of the church—and how is that purpose reflected in the way we understand, structure, and teach about what ordained ministry is?

❖

The first Christian communities had more by way of example than just the disciples who emerged as the church-building apostles. They knew two very different, and very influential, forms of leadership in religious community that shaped their thinking about how such leaders functioned.

The first, especially influential among the first Jewish Christians who found in Jesus the clear and compelling manifestation of the promised Messiah, was the model of the priestly class who devoted themselves to the service of the temple in Jerusalem. These men, identified for the role by lineage rather than a particular sense of vocation, offered the sacrifices appointed by the Hebrew scriptures within the temple precincts on a rotating basis, leaving behind home and family in order to take up a period of residence there. In addition to their own assigned times, all of the priestly families came to the temple to serve on major festivals in the Jewish liturgical year.

The priestly class in ancient Israel was "set apart" for this function in very specific and hard-edged ways. Their role was inherited; that is to say, only the members (and specifically the men) of certain families were called upon to perform this role. Within the covenant community this separation aligned the necessary functions of the work and rituals of the temple with the essentially clan-based divisions of the people. When the priests served in the temple, their service was (or at least was intended to be) wholly devoted to the temple itself, without the distractions of home, family, or other occupations.

Within the early Gentile Christian communities, groups that were not significantly shaped by the inheritance of Jewish traditions and ritual customs, a different model emerged, albeit one first fashioned by "a Hebrew born of Hebrews; as to the law, a Pharisee,"[18] namely, Saul of Tarsus. When Paul bursts on the scene filled with zeal as a planter of churches (and strenuously defending his claim to authority as an apostle despite never having seen Jesus), he does so as a person fully aware of the temple traditions—yet also determined that the reconciling message of Christ is a message not only for the Jewish people; it is for all people.

As we all learned in Sunday school, Paul sets himself apart from the concentration of apostles in Jerusalem and sets out to preach the message of the gospel in ports of call along the Mediterranean. He plants churches in places in which he finds his message welcome, whether or not the community there is significantly Jewish. In some cases, particularly in Galatia, after planting these churches he adjudicates disputes between members of the church who came from Jewish backgrounds and those who did not. As he does he announces a radically new and equal order, in which those coming into the Jesus movement from the Jewish tradition have no special claim or preferred status.

Significantly for our purposes, Paul makes no effort to identify anything like a priestly class, or to identify families who would exert dynastic control over the leadership roles in the new communities. This seems notable if only because such a model would have been both familiar and meaningful to Paul, and we may at least imagine that his reasons for departing from it must have been meaningful as well.

It doesn't seem too much of a reach to suggest that central among those reasons might have been a core theme in Paul's theology—the radical equality of all people in the new dispensation opened through the

---

18. Philippians 3:5.

cross and Resurrection. This idea, arguably the single greatest departure in Christian moral reasoning from all that had preceded it, accounts for Paul's insistence on the full and equal participation of Gentiles in the life of the first churches. It accounts as well for his critique of the distinctions that arose among the faithful in the Corinthian church along lines of wealth. It may even account for the clear evidence we have that leadership roles in the churches Paul founded were occupied by both men and women—something that sharply distinguished these communities in the cultural context of the first-century Roman Empire.

So we cannot be surprised that Paul himself lived out a pattern of ministry that did not create sharp distinctions between different ministries, other than distinctions of function:

> . . . to one is given through the Spirit the utterance of wisdom, and to another the utterance of knowledge according to the same Spirit, to another faith by the same Spirit, to another gifts of healing by the one Spirit, to another the working of miracles, to another prophecy. . . . (1 Corinthians 12:8–10)

Rather than set himself apart in a role exclusively centered on the worshiping community and maintained by their offerings—as had been the model of the priestly class in the temple—he worked among them as a laborer (as we saw earlier, as a tentmaker), earning his living in much the same way they did.

Yet that all-too-human obsession with power quickly shaped in the first Christian communities a different understanding of how ministry should work in the church. In Clement's Epistle to the Corinthians, written decades after Paul's own correspondence with that church, the argument is advanced that a godly purpose could be discerned in the ordering of different ranks of ministers, and the distribution of authority among them—an understanding itself bound up with the structuring and distribution of power. In the excerpt quoted at the beginning of this chapter, Clement buttresses his vision of a church shaped by different levels of authority with a curiously construed quote of the Septuagint rendition[19] of a verse from prophet Isaiah; from "I will make your princes peaceable, and your overseers righteous" (Isaiah 60:17, LXX), Clement delivers "I will appoint their bishops in righteousness, and their deacons in faith." It may have been convenient to his purposes, but it was hardly a faithful rendering of the text.

Harvey Cox makes an interesting point about Clement's epistle. Noting that those who find themselves drawn to a hierarchical structure of ministries in the church, culminating in the Bishop of Rome, have historically pointed to this document in support of their views, Cox draws our attention to the reason why the epistle was likely written in the first place: "If the Christians in Rome needed to persuade their Corinthian brothers and sisters about the prerogatives of those who considered themselves the successors of the apostles, clearly the Corinthians, at least the younger ones, did *not* adhere to this concept of authority at the time."[20] Exactly right. And perhaps they don't today, either.

These two contending visions of the authority of the ordained members of the church, and by extension the authority of the church itself, have remained in tension throughout the entire history of the church. That this is the case is perhaps only to be expected, in view of the competing desires we have in our lives of faith—intimacy in our relationship with God, and a sense of security from the permanence and authority of the church itself.

As a general observation, however, the human reflex for institution building and the arranging and ranking of authority has won out through the history of the church. By the third century the church had

---

19. The translation of the Hebrew Scriptures into Greek.
20. Cox, *The Future of Faith*, 90; emphasis original.

spread around the Mediterranean to North Africa, where emerged some of the most influential voices shaping the trajectory of the church's path toward the future. One of these was Cyprian (c. 200–258), an early bishop of Carthage, who late in his life learned of a priest in his diocese who had been made the executor of a wealthy man's estate. Writing to the church in Furni, where these events had taken place, Cyprian offers a view of the role of the presbyter—the priest—that is the clear inheritor of the temple priesthood in Jerusalem:

> Cyprian to the presbyters, and deacons, and people abiding at Furni, greeting. I and my colleagues who were present with me were greatly disturbed, dearest brethren, as were also our fellow-presbyters who sat with us, when we were made aware that Geminius Victor, our brother, when departing this life, had named Geminius Faustinus the presbyter executor to his will, although long since it was decreed, in a council of the bishops, that no one should appoint any of the clergy and the ministers of God executor or guardian by his will, since every one honored by the divine priesthood, and ordained in the clerical service, ought to serve only the altar and sacrifices, and to have leisure for prayers and supplications. For it is written: "No man that warreth for God entangleth himself with the affairs of this life, that he may please Him to whom he has pledged himself. . . ." The form of [this] ordination and engagement the Levites formerly observed under the law, so that when the eleven tribes divided the land and shared the possessions, the Levitical tribe, which was left free for the temple and the altar, and for the divine ministries, received nothing from that portion of the division. . . . [Instead,] that portion only cultivated the favor of God, and received tithes from the eleven tribes, for their food and maintenance, from the fruits which grew.[21]

Paul's companioning, tentmaker pastorate seems far removed indeed from this vision of ministry. The rapid growth of the church seems to

---

21. Cyprian, Epistle 65 ("To the clergy and people abiding at Furni, about Victor, who had made the presbyter Faustinus a guardian"), in *The Ante-Nicene Fathers*, ed. Alexander Roberts and James Donaldson, vol. 5 (Edinburgh: T & T Clark, reprint 1990), 367.

have tipped the scales in its early centuries toward a hierarchical shaping and distribution of authority, and an understanding of ordained ministry as something somehow separate from, and in some respects disconnected from, the rest of the faithful—that is to say, the other ministers.

Doing full justice to the unfolding of authority and the enduring tension between visions of the role and purpose of ordained ministry would require a book in itself (at least), and is not within the scope of my purpose here. It's enough to say, first, that authority itself—as a concept, not as a structure—has been understood, somewhat paradoxically to early twenty-first century Western views, as a gift of God in the life of the church; and that this gift has been expressed throughout the history of the church by a pattern of development, resistance to, and restructuring of structures of authority throughout the church's long journey.

Within the churches that emerged from the tumult of the Reformation, the working out of the exercise of authority has been a matter of considerable reflection, dissension, and occasional rebellion. This is the ineluctable result of ideas central to the Reformation that live in tension with each other: The emphasis on a personal, unmediated relationship between the individual believer and the risen Christ; the notion of the radical *spiritual* equality of all people before God, and the profound consequences of that idea for the emergence of modern democracies and the arrangement of *political* authority; and the effort on the part of Reformers to insist that the church still retained some degree of claim to authority in the life of the faithful.[22] Richard Hooker, Anglicanism's first great systematic theologian, labors in his foundational work *Of the Lawes of Ecclesiastical Polity* to make a case to England's Calvinistic Puritans that the institution of

---

22. For an excellent scholarly summary of these ideas and their working out in both ecclesial and political spheres after the Reformation, see Alec Ryrie, *Protestants: The Radicals Who Made the Modern World* (London: William Collins, 2017), published in the United States under the curiously edited title *Protestants: The Faith that Made the Modern World* (New York: Viking, 2017).

the church has both the duty and the warrant of scripture to exercise considerable authority over the governance of the spiritual lives of the faithful. The Puritans, unconvinced, were not reconciled to the Church of England.

A later reformer, John Wesley, struggles in a sermon "On Obedience to Pastors" to articulate just what is the nature of the authority of the ordained over the souls of the faithful; he ends up making a careful distinction between the claims of scripture ("things enjoined of God") and "indifferent things":

> 6. It may be of use yet again to consider, in what instances it is the duty of Christians to obey and submit themselves to those that watch over their souls. Now the things which they enjoin, must be either enjoined of God, or forbidden by him, or indifferent. In things forbidden of God, we dare not obey them; for we are to obey God rather than man. In things enjoined of God, we do not properly obey *them*, but our common Father. Therefore, if we are to obey them at all, it must be in things indifferent. The sum is, it is the duty of every private Christian, to obey his spiritual Pastor, by either doing or leaving undone anything of an indifferent nature; any thing that is in no way determined in the word of God.[23]

More recently, an effort to articulate a shared vision of authority has been at the center of conversations in the Anglican–Roman Catholic International Commission (ARCIC), established by Archbishop of Canterbury Michael Ramsey and Pope Paul VI in 1967. The product of more hopeful days in the pursuit of ecumenism, the documents issued by this continuing conversation over the course of fifty years have touched on the nature of authority (in three separate documents), as well as on the church's authority in the work of salvation.

---

23. John Wesley, "On Obedience to Pastors," preached March 18, 1785; *Wesley Center Online*, http://wesley.nnu.edu/john-wesley/the-sermons-of-john-wesley-1872 -edition/sermon-97-on-obedience-to-pastors/.

Taken together, these documents illuminate a nuanced and supple understanding of how authority works in and through the church, and how that authority is expressed by those who are its ministers. At first glance, they seem to be in keeping with the idea of "apostolic authority" seen in the section above; "The churches today are committed to receiving the one living apostolic [t]radition, to ordering their life according to it, and to transmitting it in such a way that the Christ who comes in glory will find the people of God confessing and living the faith once for all entrusted to the saints. . . ."[24]

Yet at the same time, in other places they suggest a more open and less rigid understanding of authority. Elsewhere in "The Gift of Authority," the commission notes that "The exercise of teaching authority in the church, especially in situations of challenge, requires the participation, in their distinctive ways, of the whole body of believers, not only those changed with the ministry of memory."[25] And when it comes to the question of the purpose and role of the church in the work of salvation—a topic to which we now turn—the commission has offered language that would surely have set the Council of Trent in an uproar: "The Church is . . . an instrument for the realization of God's eternal design, the salvation of humanity. *While we recognize that the Holy Spirit acts outside the community of Christians*, nevertheless it is within the [ch]urch, where the Holy gives and nurtures the new life of the Kingdom, that the [g]ospel becomes a manifest reality."[26] The question for us to consider is how best to accom-

---

24. Anglican–Roman Catholic International Commission, "The Gift of Authority (Authority in the Church III)," September 3, 1997, para. 17. AnglicanCommunion. org http://www.anglicancommunion.org/media/105245/ARCIC_II_The_Gift_of_Authority.pdf
25. Ibid., at para. 43.
26. Anglican–Roman Catholic International Commission, "Salvation and the Church," March 3, 1982, para. 28; emphasis added. AnglicanCommunion.org http://www.anglicancommunion.org/media/105239/ARCIC_II_Salvation_and_the_Church.pdf. This document also goes on to take note of the woeful impact of the abuse of authority in the history of the church: ". . . the credibility of the Church's

plish the realization and unleashing of that new life, and whether the structures of authority we have received best serves that holy purpose.

❖

Reflecting on the unsettled place of authority in ministry throughout the history of Christian community-building, we're brought up short by a fundamental question: What is the purpose of the church? This seems a strange question to ask, even, perhaps, one we are not permitted to pose. Most of us, products of the late-twentieth-century church, were raised to think of the church as having existed in the way we came to know it for years and years. But of course the church has taken many different forms and has had many different structures throughout its history. Each of those structures has suited a particular set of needs and expectations, and each has had to adapt as these needs and expectations changed.

Yet, just as with models of ministry, the purpose of the church itself has been understood—at a much higher level—in (at least) two different ways. We rarely speak of these ideas in any explicit way, yet even within small parishes there can be people who hold quite different views on the question.

Let's call the first idea the "Empire Church." It's the idea the church should have as its purpose the creation of its own realm, separate and apart from—not to say over and against—the secular world. It should have its own rules, its own structures of authority, its own ways of being. Oriented by the argument that the kingdom of heaven is a very different place from any secular regime on earth, the Empire Church regards itself as a separate and set-apart microcosm of God's kingdom on earth.

---

witness is undermined by the sins of its members, the shortcomings of its human institutions, and not least by the scandal of division. The Church is in constant need of repentance and renewal so that it can be more clearly seen for what it is: the one, holy body of Christ." Ibid. at para. 29.

It's something like an embassy: a small piece of the sovereign territory of another country, set within and fenced off from the territory of a foreign regime—in this case, the foreign territory that is the secular realm of the material world of human affairs.

The Empire Church is the church of massive campuses and grand institutions. It's the church of denominational hierarchies and national headquarters. It's the church that builds its own institutions to parallel those in the secular world—schools, hospitals, colleges, pension funds, publishing houses—providing, as much as possible, a separate path through the vale of earthly life for its members. It is, to use the terms of the introduction to this book, the "church of the firm"—the church structured along lines that paralleled, and ran contemporaneously with, the emergence of modern industrial management practices in the nineteenth century. And it waits for the day in which the triumphant return of Christ in victory vindicates its claims to sovereignty, revealing it as the true source of authority and order in what the Revelation to John speaks of as the "new earth" (Rev. 21:1).

At a theological level, the Empire Church asserts sovereign authority over all realms of human knowledge and discovery. It makes the claim—as more fully developed in works of the "radical orthodoxy" movement—that all human scientific exploration must be reconciled with, and ultimately subject to, theology, the "queen of the sciences."[27]

---

27. "Radical orthodoxy" is an umbrella term for a range of works by a number of theologians. The key text is generally regarded as *Radical Orthodoxy: A New Theology*, eds. John Milbank, Catherine Pickstock, and Graham Ward (London: Routledge, 1999). Others have included Milbank's *Theology and Social Theory* (Oxford: Blackwell, 2d ed. 2006). Milbank and Pickstock, *Truth in Aquinas* (London: Routledge, 2000); Graham Ward, *Cities of God* (London: Routledge, 2000); and Philip Blond, *Post-Secular Philosophy* (London: Routledge, 1997). A more recent example of this strain of thinking, taking a somewhat more popularizing tack, is Rod Dreher's *The Benedict Option: A Strategy for Christians in a Post-Christian World* (New York: Sentinel, 2017).

The Empire Church has deep and meaningful attractions to twenty-first century Christians. It seems to offer a refuge from the disorder and seeming abandonment of God that surrounds us. Perhaps forgetting Harvey Cox's warning against the conflation of faith and belief, we see in it the assurance that our faith is true, that God's transforming love will be revealed as the most powerful force on earth, and that the God we confess in the risen Christ will somehow protect us from what feels like the bewildering onslaught of social and cultural change.

The second idea, very different from the first, we'll call the "Incarnated Church." This church takes as its central purpose not the creation of a separate realm but a radically open engagement with the world at its doorstep. Placing at the center of its identity its claim to be the risen body of Christ in the world, it engages the world as Christ did—not by sitting at a safe remove in the temple precincts, but by seeking constantly to collapse all the barriers and all the invented distinctions that separate God's children from each other and from God.

If the metaphor for the Empire Church is an embassy of God, that of the Incarnated Church is, perhaps not surprisingly, a breathing organism. Drawing in its breath, it gathers the faithful around word and sacrament to share the reconciling message of the gospel, teach the disciplines of discipleship, and strengthen all of its members for the work of ministry beyond its walls. Exhaling, it sends these ministers, lay and ordained, out into a hostile, secular world, to share by word and example the message of God's offer of redemption and reconciliation in Christ.

The Incarnated Church does not seek to create for itself a protected space, remembering that the Christ it proclaims wins victory over evil and death not through separation and strength but through radical vulnerability—ultimately, the stark vulnerability of Jesus nailed to the cross.[28] Seeing

---

28. A central text for this idea of the church is the late William Placher's *Narratives of a Vulnerable God: Christ, Theology, and Scripture* (Louisville, Ky.: Westminster John

its purpose through this theological lens, and patterning itself after that understanding of the Incarnation, it seeks to do the work of carrying out the work of discipleship through direct—and vulnerable—engagement with the world. It works to meet the culture on its own ground and on its own terms, in order to bring it to accept the gift of faith and the offer of reconciliation made in Christ.

The Incarnated Church leaves behind the safety of institutions and structures to follow the example of the earthly ministry of Jesus. It is the church of Catholic Worker houses and street ministries to the homeless. It is the church of worship incorporating contemporary culture and music, the church that eagerly incorporates new technology and media, the church that seeks to be present in the world rather than set apart from the world. To use the terms of the introduction, it is the "church of the commons"—a work of peers united in a common purpose and governed by collective accountability to a set of standards and practices. The Incarnated Church inspires us by its zeal, its radical openness, its vulnerability, its willingness to embrace risk in living out discipleship. And because of that risk, it frightens us a little, too.

Of course, these models are broadly drawn generalizations. They characterize, rather than categorize, different ways in which the church—theologians, leaders, and people—have understood its purpose down through the generations. Each of them has strengths and weakness. It's not central to my purpose to explore these in detail; rather, I offer a sketch of these models not so much as critiques but as ways for understanding different (even sometimes seemingly contradictory) expressions of an entity we call "the church," and to focus our thinking as we seek to plot a

Knox, 1994).

path for the church into a future being shaped by new and unprecedented economic, cultural, and social shifts.

With these two very different visions of the church's purpose and place in the world, we have a frame of reference with which to assess which models of ministry might be best aligned with God's call of discipleship amidst the challenges we face in the future. Many, many individual parishes struggling with survival today were conceived as expressions of the Empire Church—large physical structures, staffed by a team of professional clergy, creating a separate realm of authority within the communities they served. No longer able to support the costs of maintaining those physical and institutional structures, they are facing the difficult challenge of giving up the assumptions on which they were built and embracing a new understanding of what the church is—an understanding more closely patterned on the ideas at the heart of the Incarnated Church. That shift can be disorienting; it can feel like a loss. But it may instead be a time of renewal, and vitality—a return to the roots of ministry.

I want to offer the thought that the two models of ministry we sketched out at the beginning of this book—the Standard Model and an alternative, bivocational model of ministry—have their parallels in these two visions of what the church's purpose is and how it lives in the world. And—not surprisingly—as we increasingly find ourselves shifting away from the days of the Empire Church and toward (or perhaps back to) an Incarnated Church, we will also find ourselves shifting increasingly away from what we have come to regard as the "Standard Model" for ministry and toward a "bivocational model"—which will have implications, as we have seen throughout this book, not just for the ordained ministers of the church but for all people of faith, for the congregations in which they gather, and for the ultimately contingent denominational structures we have shaped. To see what I mean somewhat more graphically, let's set the two models of both church and ministry in a 2-by-2 matrix.

TABLE 1: ALTERNATIVE MODELS OF CHURCH AND MINISTRY

IDEA OF CHURCH	IDEA OF MINISTRY
Empire Church • A separate realm; establishing the "City of God" in the midst of the secular • Interlocking set of institutions create an alternative path through the world for the faithful • Authority is shaped and distributed by institutional structure • High claim of sovereignty over human discovery and inquiry • The "church of the firm"	**Standard Model** • Hierarchically arranged structures of power expressed by means of a professionalized ordained ministry • Authority of those in ordered ministries derives from credentialing (degrees, sacramental ordination, "certificates on the wall"), shaped in turn by institutions of the church • Clear distinction between role of ordained minister and place of the laity • Life of the community has a sacramental focus, centered on what distinguishes the ordained and lay members.
Incarnated Church • No (or limited) separation from world outside the church • Institutions are flatter, less hierarchical, shaped by purpose in view • Authority arises from charism more than from office or order of ministry • Engagement with the discoveries of human inquiry • The "church of the commons"	**Bivocational Ministry** • Ordination disconnected from conferral of professional status • Authority in Christian community flows from the endowment of spiritual gifts • Authority and responsibility in the community more equitably shared, along lines of gifts and skills • Life of the community has a missiological focus, centered on the shared tasks of discipleship

The Upshot: Implications of the Shifting Models of Church and Ministry

In chapter 2 we revisited the categories of congregation size suggested by Arlin Rothauge, recalling the different systems associated with each; and we noted Alice Mann's observations about the tendency for congregations to plateau as they try to grow from one size to another. Rothauge's insight was that differently sized congregations comprise systems that work in different ways; Mann's insight was that relationship between size and system is a key reason that congregations generally experience difficulty in trying to grow to such an extent that they cross the border from one size to another, because those systems become inscribed in the culture and ethos of a community. What we have tried to add to this set of ideas is the notion that the same holds true of congregations that are contracting. In their case, however, crossing the boundary from one congregational size to another may not be the result of effort and design on the part of the community, but of the cultural and economic forces that bring change upon congregations regardless of any choice on their part. And the result of that forced change, "downshifting" from the systems associated with one size to those associated with another, can be bewildering and confusing.

The models of church I've described above turn out not to be implicated with the size-driven categories of congregational type suggested by Rothauge and Mann. How a congregation understands the overall purpose and vision of the universal church is more a function of its culture, its narrative history, and its traditions. If at some point—likely in the 1950s or 1960s—a church built a large campus with classrooms and gathering spaces, the members of that church now confront a physical manifestation of the claims of the Empire Church every time they come to worship, no matter how many (or how few) others will be joining them.

The challenge of shifting from the systems associated with one size of congregational life to the systems associated with another is a challenge associated with *numerical* growth—specifically, growth in Sunday attendance. But when it comes to shifting between the two different models of how the church understands its purpose—the shift from empire church to incarnational church—the challenge is associated instead with *spiritual* growth. It's a *qualitative* rather than a quantitative change. It's bound up in the challenge set before all members of the community to take more seriously in their daily lives the claims of the call to discipleship, to understand themselves as ministers of the church in the world no matter where they spend most of their time in the world, and to renew and deepen their shared commitment to each other and to God as sharers in the responsibility of the church's mission in the world.

That growth involves new ways of thinking about and living out the roles of ordained and lay people in the world. A bivocational understanding of ministry, imbued as it is with the ethos of the incarnated church, understands that just as the church must be the open and accessible point of conversation and connection between God's purposes and the world's needs, so all those who share in the ministry of the church must reflect on how the gifts with which the Spirit has uniquely equipped them have prepared them to be ministers of the church in the world—the ordained, no less (and no differently) from the lay folks.

To grow into this church, a church of greater openness, greater engagement, greater vulnerability—and, perhaps it should be said, less pretension—is not easy. It will mean setting aside some of the comforts and assurances that came with the understanding of the church's importance in the social and cultural scales of the secular world. It will mean, for the ordained members of our communities, setting aside the expectations of preferment and distinction that the old model of church raised us to believe were ours by right—the fruit of the idea that ordination somehow signaled and rewarded one's superior spiritual qualities. And it will mean, for the lay ministers of our congregations, an end to the comforting and transactional notion that the work of ministry was something we delegate to the minister of the community—the "hired Christian"—and embracing an understanding of ministry shared much more fully, and much more equally, on all those gifted in baptism by the Spirit.

Chapter 5

We Can Get There From Here

I was standin' outside Sutherland's IGA store one mornin' when I heard a flivver approachin' down the street toward me.

"Which way to Millinocket?"

"Well, you can go west to the next intersection; get on to the turnpike; go north, through the tollgate at Augusta. When you come to that intersection . . . well, no. . . .

"You can keep right on this tar road—it changes to dirt now and again—just keep the river on your left. You'll come to the crossroads and . . . let me see. . . .

"Then again, you can take that scenic coastal route that the tourists use. And after you get to Bucksport . . . well, let me see now . . . Millinocket. . . .

"Come to think of it, you can't get there from here!"[29]

The Christian church has come a very long way indeed from the days of the apostle Paul. It spread around the Mediterranean littoral as a source of hope carried by the preaching of the first apostles and by the songs of merchants plying the ports where trade flourished in the

---

29. Marshall Dodge and Bob Bryan as "Bert and I." Best heard at https://www.you tube.com/watch?v=sIJBUZm1HoY. Bryan, incidentally, went on to be ordained in the Episcopal Church.

ancient world. Opposed by the forces of the Roman Empire, persecuted by the whims of emperors, it later became the faith of the empire—and then was blamed by some for the empire's collapse and downfall. Enduring throughout the medieval period, it spread throughout the worlds of Europe, Africa, and the Near East throughout the following centuries, surviving even the shattering break between the churches of the west and east. It became part of the power structure of the (not accidentally named) Holy Roman Empire, animated the emergence of the modern era through the ideas of the Reformation, and was spread across the planet by the efforts of missionaries—who were often effectively agents of, and often supported by, the emerging power of nation-states. It has taken on many forms, adapted to countless circumstances, risen to many challenges, and built institutions for good (and not-so-good) purposes.

The cultural circumstances in which the church finds itself today, however, are unique. They are unprecedented in the depth of the challenge they pose to the message the church offers. It's not that the human quest for the spiritual has somehow come to an end; but it may be, as Harvey Cox has suggested, that after centuries of building religious institutions we are leaving an "age of belief" and entering instead upon an "age of faith." This is an age in which the sense of the possibility of the sacred is pursued not through institutional structures of belief (that is, through religious traditions), but through seeking out and holding onto those communities and ideas that strengthen and deepen the experience of faith. Perhaps it is true, as Cox observes, that "faith, rather than beliefs, is once again becoming" the defining quality of Christianity.[30]

But if that is indeed the case, what are we to do with the structures of belief we have created—and the patterns of ministry inherent to them?

---

30. Harvey Cox, *The Future of Faith*, 223.

These questions are by no means new. As we saw in chapter 3, as early as the mid-twentieth century Dietrich Bonhoeffer was posing questions about a future characterized by "religionless Christianity." And nearly fifty years ago, writing in the scholarly journal *Theology* while teaching at Lincoln Theological College in England—of which he would later be the warden—Alec Graham asked bluntly in the title of an article, "Should the Ordained Ministry Now Disappear?"[31] Graham pointed out that while the church had historically found some form of ordained ministry to be needful, the cataclysms of world wars of the twentieth century had caused many to doubt. They doubted because of resistance to authority and hierarchy, because of resentment and rejection of the social status given to clergy, and because (Graham thought most trenchantly) the idea of the "priesthood of all believers" had finally caught up with the life of the church—through widespread literacy, the spread of education, and "the wider spread of the experience of responsibility."[32]

In this third critique Graham saw the thin end of a wedge that, in the end, would call into question the theological status and validity of the very idea of ordained ministry in the church of the future. That did not mean—and does not mean—that the claims of the Christian faith were (and are) any less true. It does mean, however, that the endurance and advance of that truth into the future may not depend on ordained ministries the way they've historically been understood.

In such a moment it's both helpful and reassuring to remember that we have not always been arranged and structured as we currently are. While in times of change and tumult our greatest desire for the church might be that it be a source of comfort and permanence, that is not a

---

31. A. A. K. Graham, "Should the Ordained Ministry now Disappear?" *Theology* 71:576 (1968), 242–250.
32. Ibid., 245.

stance for disciples to take. What is unchangeable and permanent is the God we have come to know in the gospel message. And the God we have come to know, and who calls us in baptism to be disciples, is restless; "his going forth is sure as the dawn" (Hosea 6:3, RSV).

What shape, then, might ordained ministry take in these changed circumstances? How might it evolve to serve the needs of an age of faith, as distinct from the age of belief that seems now to be closing?

Bishop Graham (as he later became), in that fifty-year-old essay, pointed to three qualities, or perhaps characteristics, that together gave shape to a new sort of identity for those ordained—an identity, not of authority, but of *representation*. In this vision, the significance of the ordained ministry is not that it lays claim to a certain kind of specialized authority in the church, but rather that it seeks to represent within the community of the faithful what a life of discipleship looks like—and, in doing so, represents to all members of the community the possibility inherent in their own lives to be disciples as well.

Bishop Graham offered his own views on the three characteristics associated with this identity of representation, which I will try to do justice to here—while at the same time suggesting how they align with the vision of bivocational ministry this book has tried to describe.

The first is the quality of *displaying* the life of a disciple—the "total response demanded by Christ . . . to follow and obey." We are taught early in our walk of faith the stories of the disciples leaving behind their worldly occupations to join the Jesus movement; but we are also reminded by Paul's example that after the events of Christ's death, resurrection, and ascension, and until his promised return, the necessities of worldly life are not beneath the dignity of disciples. As Graham says,

> the response of the ordained minister to . . . vocation is not made in order [to] provide an edifying example of renunciation. . . . It means that certain Christians publicly, unambiguously, with particular solemnity,

at a mature age, renew that total dedication to their master which . . . *should characterize the life of every Christian.* . . .[33]

The bivocational minister exemplifies this function of displaying the life of discipleship both in the worshiping community *and* in the place in which disciples are called to dwell—not in a separate realm called the church, but in the world God has made and in which we are called as God's co-creators to build the kingdom. Such an understanding of ordination is oriented principally on demonstrating the full possibility of discipleship in church and world, not on an expression of gifts limited to the realm of the church.

Second, the ordained-as-representative exhibits the quality of *enabling*—"the explicit and clear display should have the effect . . . of enabling [the church's] members to see more clearly what is meant by Christian discipleship *and to pursue it more purposefully.*"[34] This quality, as we saw in chapter 2, is central to the qualities of leadership that strong bivocational pastors demonstrate within their communities—the ability to discern the gifts of each member of community, connect these gifts to the needs of the community, and encourage the expression of those gifts to the fullest extent possible. Where our understanding of this quality differs from Bishop Graham's is on the matter of how this sort of leadership is expressed. Graham's notion is that the "enabling influence" of the ordained is in some way associated with being "ordained to full-time service."[35] But I see no prevailing reason why this must be the case; and indeed, in the bivocational congregations I have witnessed firsthand, the enabling quality of leadership exhibited by ordained ministers is often linked to, rather than inhibited by, their work in two worlds. Said in

33. Ibid., 248; emphasis added.
34. Ibid.; emphasis added.
35. Ibid.

different words, it is not only in the setting or work of the church that Christians function as ministers.

The third and last of Bishop Graham's characteristics of a representative ministry is the quality of *involving*—in the sense of "involving the whole church" in each activity undertaken. On this point I offer a rather different understanding from Bishop Graham's original meaning. He offers the idea of the ordained minister having a unique responsibility to involve the whole church in all of the activities, all of the work, all of the calendar entries in a given day. The sense here is of one person being, and bringing, the whole of the church into all that they do:

> Ideally, the whole church should be caring and proclaiming, worshipping and reconciling, but this cannot be effectively done only by Christians in the course of their daily occupations. Particular people are, therefore, largely set free from other cares and duties in order that their time and energy may be devoted to these ends.[36]

Bishop Graham here indulges in a somewhat sweeping generalization that has the effect of justifying the existence of a separate and distinct realm—I am almost inclined to describe it as a club—for a "particular people" called ordained ministers. But the life of congregations tells a different story. There are countless examples of people who do excellent work visiting the sick, leading the study of scripture, "caring and proclaiming, worshipping and reconciling," without the benefit of—nor any need for—ordination. And every one of us who is ordained—at least, every honest one of us—will acknowledge that there were fellow-ministers in our communities who did at least some of these things, things essential to Christian community, better than we do.

The quality of involvement is central to bivocational ministry as well, but in a way different from Bishop Graham's notion. It is rather the idea

---

36. Ibid., 249.

that all members of the Christian community are called to involve the life of the church, the values of the church, and the claims of the church in all aspects of their lives—both inside and outside the church. The ordained leader of a bivocational congregation is called both to model this manner of discipleship and to inculcate it within the faith community by lifting up examples of all in the community who do it in their lives as well. Involvement in this sense is closely linked to the notion of *integrity*—the idea that our lives of faith are not meant to be lived in a compartmentalized way, with some aspects given to church and the rest given to other claims, but with our whole lives—mind, heart, soul, and strength—devoted to loving God, and expressing that love through all that we do, wherever we do it.

The question that remains for us is, how? What is the path? And how will we know if we are making progress toward this objective?

I conclude this short work on bivocational ministry by suggesting some specific measures we might implement to increase the number of people in ordained ministry prepared to take on a bivocational role; to strengthen the work of congregations seeking to explore this model as a path toward their future; and to expand both the capacity and the willingness of denominational polities to acknowledge and support this approach to the future ministry of the church.

I. IDENTIFYING BIVOCATIONAL PASTORS

WHAT COULD WE DO?	WHAT WOULD SUCCESS LOOK LIKE?
• Actively recruit engaged lay leaders to consider ordination for ministries that would be consistent with remaining in their present professional roles.	• A steady increase in the percentage of candidates for ordination who continue working in secular roles while preparing for ordination. • A gradual move away from the dominant norm of three-year-in-residence divinity school and toward a model more like the service of reservists in the armed forces; occasional periods of intensive training interspersed with routine engagements with field work or experiential education. • Work toward a goal of between 25 and 30 percent of all candidates for ordination preparing along these lines.
• Help those currently ordained to expand their skill base to prepare for work in secular employment alongside their ordained ministry.	• Create partnerships with institutions of higher education to provide access to training programs for currently ordained ministers. • Develop and incentivize professional development tracks for those presently in full-time ordained positions to hone their skills for work outside the church.

2. STRENGTHENING BIVOCATIONAL CONGREGATIONS

WHAT COULD WE DO?	WHAT WOULD SUCCESS LOOK LIKE?
• Provide focused training and coaching to develop leadership skills among lay leaders.	• The percentage of lay members of a congregation actively engaged in the life of the community rises to between 40 and 50 percent of all members. • Bivocational congregations develop network relationships between themselves—within and across denominational traditions—to share ideas, best practices, and training opportunities.
• Help congregations explore received understandings and expectations of ordained ministry, and how this inheritance has shaped the culture and ethos of their community.	• Workshops provide congregations with tools for setting the ordained ministry in historical context and for bringing to the surface narrative histories and implicit expectations placed on ordained ministers. • Congregations develop a practice of assessing how responsibilities are shared between ordained and lay ministers, and of aligning authority with delegated responsibility.

3. REORIENTING POLITIES TOWARD BIVOCATIONAL POSSIBILITIES

WHAT COULD WE DO?	WHAT WOULD SUCCESS LOOK LIKE?
• Normalize bivocational congregations as within the mainstream of congregational life, rather than regarding them as an outlier or "less-than" form expression of church.	• Greater participation of both lay and ordained leaders of bivocational congregations in governing structures of the polity. • The emergence of pathways for preparation to ordained ministry that reflect the realities of the demands placed on those working in secular employment. • Candidates for the top leadership of polity-level structures, in both ordained and lay roles, emerge from bivocational congregations.
• Broaden the understanding and communication of gifts sought in those who offer themselves for consideration as candidates for ordained ministry to include those who remain engaged in jobs outside the church.	• An increase in the percentage of candidates for ordination that continue working in secular roles while preparing for ordination. • A clear set of professional qualifications for, and experience in, work outside the church is seen as a prerequisite for new candidates for ordination.

• Identify lay and ordained leaders of congregations that have successfully developed a bivocational ethos and empower them to be coaches and trainers for others.	• Emergence of lay and ordained coaching teams within and (ideally) across denominational lines. • The work of these teams is supported with resources from polity-level structures.

Displaying, enabling, involving—these are the qualities of Christian witness that can communicate with the changed cultural circumstances around us, and speak to the world we inhabit on its own terms. They are qualities that push against arguments for special status and claims for distinction. They live out in our ministry the radical equality of all humans before God that is the scandalous idea at the center of the gospel message—the gospel we are meant not only to proclaim, but to live by. And they help us to give shape and substance to an understanding of ordained ministry, and a vision of a flourishing church, prepared to walk with God into God's future.

If we look for and lift up those members of our communities who quietly and confidently demonstrate these qualities, if we reimagine the purpose and function of ordained ministry in the light of these characteristics, and if we renew our understanding of God's purposes in the larger church by seeing these qualities as the spiritual gifts God has given us to build with, we can—and will—get there from here.

Acknowledgments

Only after I began writing this book did I realize how many of the ordained people who have most significantly influenced my faith and my life—both by friendship and example—were themselves bivocational pastors. One of them, my sixth-grade teacher Jerry Smith, is the first person you meet in this book. Others have been teachers (Robert L. Hammett, Peter Gomes, Anne Garrison, Isobel Blyth), social entrepreneurs (John H. Finley IV, Debbie Little Wyman, and John Thomas), investment gurus (Robert G. Windsor), scholars and academic leaders (Sarah Drummond, Bryan Hehir), civil servants (Howard Simpson), even elected officials (John Danforth). I have no doubt that because of their examples, the idea of growing into such a life in ministry was made real to me.

The many churches and faith communities I visited in the course of my research, and the ordained ministers who unfailingly gave generously of the one rarest resource in their lives—time—were immensely helpful in helping me think through why some congregations make bivocational expressions of ministry work, while others find it hard to do. They were welcoming, patient, willing to share stories of both success and failure, and glad to know that there might be others in places out there like them. There are.

Mark Wastler and Sarah Drummond read earlier drafts of this work and provided helpful and insightful comments on what was good, what wasn't, and what was missing. What's good about this work is largely in their debt; what isn't is down to me. Milton Brasher-Cunningham extensively and carefully edited the first draft of the complete manuscript, and improved it greatly not just through his work but through his questions. Rachel Erdman provided a painstaking copyedit of the final manuscript, and saved me from many errors of both commission and omission.

This book is dedicated to the people of Saint John's Church in Newtonville, Massachusetts. We have a long history together, and a community that knows you well and yet still loves you is a very great treasure indeed. Saint John's gave me the gift of a sabbatical in the spring of 2016 to begin the research that led to this book. Well beyond that benefit, however, they have taught me most of what I know about life in Christian community, and especially about the profound significance of the Christian virtue of hospitality. No words of mine could ever sound the depths of my gratitude to that beloved community.

Further Reading

The nature of the ministry of the church, the way in which it should be constituted and ordered, and the source and character of the authority dispensed by those who are ordained has a long history of examination and argument among Christian writers. Practically every major writer in the Christian tradition has addressed the question in some way, not least because it is a short distance from this question to the broader question of the authority the church claims for its teaching and doctrine.

It is impossible to provide here a comprehensive bibliography of writings on the question; among other things, such an undertaking would likely double the length of what is intended to be a small book. Instead I offer below a range of sources on the nature and purpose of ordained ministry in the church, covering a broad spectrum of views across the history of the church. There is no agreement to be found among these writings—merely a demonstration of the considerable breadth of ideas that have been offered on what the ministry is, and a sense of how those ideas have not infrequently been advanced in the interests of other, larger arguments about the nature and purpose of the church.

Perspectives on Ministry in the Early Church

Ignatius of Antioch, "Epistle to the Smyrnaeans," esp. chapter 8 ("Let nothing be done without the bishop") and chapter 9 ("Honor the bishop"), in *The Ante-Nicene Fathers*, vol. 1, trans. Alexander Roberts and James Donaldson; Alexander Roberts, James Donaldson, and A. Cleveland Coxe, eds. *New Advent,* http://www.newadvent.org/fathers/0109.htm.

Irenaeus, "Against Heresies," esp. Book 4, chapter 26 ("The treasure hid in the scriptures is Christ; the true exposition of the scriptures is to be found in the church alone"), in *The Ante-Nicene Fathers*, vol. 1, trans. Alexander Roberts and Rambaut; Alexander Roberts, James Donaldson, and A. Cleveland Coxe, eds. *New Advent,* http://www.newadvent.org /fathers/0103.htm.

Tertullian, "On Exhortation to Chastity," esp. chapter 7, in *The Ante-Nicene Fathers*, vol. 4, trans. S. Thelwall; Alexander Roberts, James Donaldson, and A. Cleveland Coxe, eds. *New Advent,* http://www.new advent.org/fathers/0405.htm.

Cyprian, "Epistle 9 (on the limits of the authority of presbyters)," and "Epistle 65 (on the prohibition from involvement in secular matters of presbyters)," in *The Ante-Nicene Fathers*, vol. 5, trans. Robert Ernest Wallis; Alexander Roberts, James Donaldson, and A. Cleveland Coxe, eds. *New Advent* http://www.newadvent.org/fathers/0506.htm.

John N. Collins, *Diakonia: Re-interpreting the Ancient Sources.* Oxford: Oxford University Press, 1990.

Michael J. Wilkins and Terence Paige, eds., *Worship, Theology, and Ministry in the Early Church* [Essays in honor of Ralph P. Martin]. Sheffield: Sheffield Academic Press / Journal for the Study of the New Testament, Supplement Series 87, 1992.

Medieval and Early Modern Thinking on Ministry

Everett U. Crosby, *Bishop and Chapter in Twelfth-Century England: A Study of the "Mensa Episcopalis."* Cambridge: Cambridge University Press, 1994.

Richard Hooker, *Of the Lawes of Ecclesiastical Politie*, Book 5, at 76 ("Of the nature of that ministry which serveth for performance of divine duties in the Church of God, and how happiness not eternal only but also temporal doth depend upon it"), and 77 ("Of power given unto men to execute that heavenly office; of the gift of the Holy Ghost in ordination; and whether conveniently the power of order may be sought or sued for"), in *The Works of that Learned and Judicious Divine, Mr. Richard Hooker: with an Account of His Life and Death*, ed. John Keble. Oxford: Clarendon Press, 1876; available at http://www/anglicanhistory.org /hooker/

Martin Luther, "That a Christian Assembly or Congregation has the Right and Power to Judge all Teaching and to Call, Appoint, and Dismiss Teachers, Established and Proved by Scripture" (1523), trans. Eric W. and Ruth C. Gritsch. *Luther's Works*, vol. 39. Philadelphia: Fortress Press, 1970.

————, "Concerning the Ministry" (1523), trans. Conrad Bergendoff. *Luther's Works,* vol. 40. Philadelphia: Muhlenberg Press, 1958.

————, "The Keys" (1530), trans. Earl Beyer and Conrad Bergendoff. *Luther's Works,* vol. 40. Philadelphia: Muhlenberg Press, 1958.

Jeannine Olson, "Calvin and the Diaconate," *Liturgy* 2 (1982): 78-83.

Thinking on the Nature of Ministry and Secular Work in the Modern Age

Dietrich Bonhoeffer, Letter to Eberhard Bethge, April 30, 1944; in *Dietrich Bonhoeffer Works*, vol. 8 ("Letters and Papers from Prison"), eds. Christian Gremmels, Eberhard Bethge, Renate Bethge, Ilse Tödt, and John W. de Gruchy; trans. Isabel Best, Lisa E. Dahill, Reinhard Krauss, and Nancy Lukens. Minneapolis, Minn.: Fortress Press, 2010.

A[ndrew]. A[lexander]. K[enneth]. Graham, "Shall the Ordained Ministry now Disappear?" *Theology*, vol. 71, issue 576 (1968), 242–250.

Kurt Marquart, "The Gospel Ministry: Distinctions Within and Without," unpublished mss., March 13, 1995; https://archive.org/details/TheGospelMinistryByKurtMarquart1995.

John Piper, *Brothers, We Are Not Professionals: A Plea to Pastors for Radical Ministry*. Nashville, Tenn.: B & H Publishing Group, 2013.

Michael Ramsey, *The Christian Priest Today*. London: SPCK, 1972; Cambridge, Mass.: Cowley Publications, 1985 (reprint).

Dorothy L. Sayers, "Why Work?" (speech in Eastbourne, U.K., April 23, 1942), in *Letters to a Diminished Church: Passionate Arguments for the Relevance of Christian Doctrine*. Nashville, Tenn.: Thomas Nelson, 2004.

Ministry in America

E. Brooks Holifield, *God's Ambassadors: The Christian Clergy in America*. Grand Rapids, Mich.: William B. Eerdmans, 2007.

Donald M. Scott, *From Office to Profession: The New England Ministry, 1750-1850*. Philadelphia: University of Pennsylvania Press, 1978.

Timothy F. Sedgwick, *The Making of Ministry*. Boston, Mass.: Cowley Publications, 1993.

William H. Willimon, *Pastor: The Theology and Practice of Ordained Ministry*. Nashville, Tenn.: Abingdon Press, 2002.

Recent writing on Bivocational Ministry

A number of volumes have appeared in recent years exploring the phenomenon of bivocational ministry. Typically approaching it as an anomaly in need of justification, these volumes have often related specific case studies or made a case for accepting the possibility of a bivocational approach to ministry within a specific denominational context. Rarely if ever, however, do they regard the phenomenon of bivocational ministry as a matter describing more than the employment status of the ordained pastor. It is perhaps indicative of the view held of bivocational ministry by the publishing outlets of denominational traditions that many of these works have been self-published, availing themselves of new digital publishing tools. They include:

Denis W. Bickers, *The Bivocational Pastor: Two Jobs, One Ministry.* Kansas City, Mo.: Nazrene Publishing House, 2014.

————, *The Art and Practice of Bivocational Ministry: A Pastor's Guide.* Kansas City, Mo.: Beacon Hill Press, 2013.

————, *The Work of the Bivocational Minister.* Valley Forge, Penn.: Judson Press, 2007.

Doug Black, Jr., *Marathon: A Manual for Bivocational Ministry.* Self-Published, 2014.

Steve Clapp, Ron Finney, and Angela Zimmerman, *Preaching, Planning, and Plumbing: The Implications of Bivocational Ministry for the Church and for You—Discovering God's Call to Service and Joy.* London: Christian Community Press, 1999.

Luther M. Dorr, *The Bivocational Pastor.* Nashville, Tenn.: Sunday School Publishing Board [National Baptist Convention], 1988.

Hugh Halter, *BiVo: A Modern-Day Guide for Bi-Vocational Saints.* Littleton, Colo.: Missio Publishing, 2013.

Lamar Herndon, *Constructing Blue Collar Leaders in a White Collar World.* Winter Park, Fl.: Legacy Book Publishing, 2015.

James W. Highland, Serving as a Bivocational Pastor. Newburgh, Ind.: Newburgh Press, 2013.

Rosario Picardo, *Ministry Makeover: Recovering a Theology for Bi-Vocational Service in the Church*. Eugene, Ore.: Wipf & Stock, 2015.

Warren Siebert, *The Calling of a Part-Time Pastor: A Guidebook for Small-Church Leaders*. Grand Rapids, Mich. and Nashville, Tenn.: WestBow Press, 2016.

Tim Westrom and Becca Westrom, *Help for the Bivocational Pastor: Thriving in your Multifaceted Calling*. Self-Published, 2017.

Commons-Based Organization

Yochai Benkler, *The Wealth of Networks: How Social Production Transforms Markets and Freedom*. New Haven, Conn.: Yale University Press, 2006; full text available at http://www.benkler.org/Benkler_Wealth_Of _Networks.pdf

David Bollier, *Think Like a Commoner: A Short Introduction to the Life of the Commons*. Gabriola Island, BC: New Society Publishers, 2014.